e-Governance in Andhra Pradesh

Published by
ACADEMIC FOUNDATION
in association with

Institute of Public Enterprise

ABOUT THE AUTHORS

R.K. Mishra, Director, Institute of Public Enterprise (IPE), Hyderabad, has studied, researched and taught at the University of Rajasthan, London Business School, SDA Bocconi, University of Bradford and International Center for Promotion of Enterprises. He is a Visiting Professor at Maison Des Sciences De L' Hommes, Faculty of Economics University of Ljubljana and UiTM, Malaysia. He has handled assignments from UNDESA, OECD, ADB, Cabinet Secretariat, Government of India, Commonwealth Secretariat, various ministries of Government of India, state governments and public enterprises. He has guided doctoral research and taught at the MBA programmes in several universities in India and abroad. His areas of interest include: corporate governance, corporate social responsibility (CSR), enterprise management and public policy.

A. Sridhar Raj is an Assistant Professor at IPE, Hyderabad. He has done his Masters Degree in Public Administration and has completed his PhD in the area of Training and Development. He is involved in research, consultancy and training in the area of public sector enterprises. His areas of interest are: governance, citizen services, citizen charters, policy formulation and policy execution. He has published cases pertaining to government departments. Before joining IPE, he was with Centre for Good Governance and ICFAI.

A.N.K. Prasanna Anjaneyulu has 14 years of teaching experience at Engineering and Post Graduate colleges. He was Associate Member of Technologist at Institution of Engineers (India), Kolkata and worked at Engineering Staff College of India (The Forum of Institution of Engineers), Hyderabad, before joining IPE. He has presented research papers, participated in national and international conferences, and has published articles in national and international journals. His areas of specialisation include: enterprise resource planning, software testing, data warehousing, data mining, web mining, relational database management system and programming languages.

K.V. Anantha Kumar, Assistant Professor at IPE, Hyderabad, is Mechanical Engineer and MBA (Marketing) from Osmania University. He was awarded PhD in 2006 for his research work on “Marketing Strategies of Life Insurance Corporation of India: A Comparative Study”. In his 16 years experience, he taught Operational Research, Statistics for Management, Operations Management, Marketing Management, Marketing Research, Decision Analysis, Product Management and Total Quality Management. He has participated and presented papers in a number of conferences. Dr Ananth is on the editorial board of “Drishtikon”, a journal enlisted in Ulrich, Cabell's Directory and EBSCO. His areas of interest include: micro insurance, customer relationship management, customer satisfaction, evaluation studies.

e-Governance in Andhra Pradesh

A Case of Mee Seva

R.K. Mishra
A. Sridhar Raj
A.N.K. Prasanna Anjaneyulu
K.V. Anantha Kumar

ACADEMIC FOUNDATION
NEW DELHI
www.academicfoundation.org

First published in 2016
by

ACADEMIC FOUNDATION
4772-73 / 23 Bharat Ram Road, (23 Ansari Road),
Darya Ganj, New Delhi - 110 002 (India).
Phones : 23245001 / 02 / 03 / 04.
Fax : +91-11-23245005.
E-mail : books@academicfoundation.com
www.academicfoundation.org

in association with
Institute of Public Enterprise, Hyderabad.

Disclaimer:
The findings/views/opinions expressed in this book are solely those of the authors and do not necessarily reflect the views of the publisher.

E-governance in Andhra Pradesh : a case of Mee Seva / R.K. Mishra ... [et al.].
p. cm.
Includes bibliographical references (p.).
ISBN 9789332701663

1. Internet in public administration--India--Andhra Pradesh. 2. Web services--India--Andhra Pradesh. 3. Mee Seva (Project : Andhra Pradesh, India)--Evaluation. I. Mishra, R. K., 1948- II. Title: Electronic-governance in Andhra Pradesh.

DDC 352.38028546780954 23

Typeset, Printed and bound by The Book Mint, New Delhi.
www.thebookmint.in

CONTENTS

LIST OF TABLES AND FIGURES

Tables

Figures

Preface

The National e-Governance Plan (NeGP) formulated by the Government of India (GoI) takes a comprehensive view of e-Governance as a gateway for providing hassle-free services for citizens. The plan aims to bring convergence among various departments through technology-enabled processes for better service delivery for the citizens.

In sync with the nationwide initiatives being taken by the GoI, the Government of Andhra Pradesh (GoAP) too has taken specific initiatives towards creating a better interface between the government and the citizens. The aim of these initiatives was to simplify the government processes and integrate them with technology for the wider reach of the citizens. The GoAP has already set up in place the Andhra Pradesh State Wide Area Network (APSWAN), AP State Data Centre (SDC), e-Seva Centres, APOnline Centres, and Common Service Centers (CSCS). A major step was taken by the government to knit all these initiatives together to harness their benefits for providing better services to the citizens in the form of Mee Seva.

The Hon'ble Chief Minister of Andhra Pradesh launched Mee Seva in the district of Chittoor on 4 November 2011 and later the same was rolled out in other districts in a phased manner. Mee Seva is a gateway which provides electronic delivery of government services to the citizens within a given timeframe. During the transactions, a high level of transparency and convenience to the citizens is ensured. The project works on an 'integrated service delivery model' to provide a single point 'easier and faster' entry for a wide range of services to the citizens.

The Institute of Public Enterprise (IPE) has undertaken a study to evaluate Mee Seva in all the districts of Andhra Pradesh (AP). The study found that the citizens have appreciated Mee Seva and the overall satisfaction of Mee Seva services among the citizens is as high as 63 per cent. The high satisfaction levels in relation to Mee Seva indicate that it can be scaled up and rolled out in the entire country for delivering services to citizens in an easy way.

Mee Seva project is a landmark initiative by the GoAP, with the potential to pave the way for transparent, responsive, and accountable governance in the state. Some areas have been identified for strengthening its implementation—stabilising field operations, strengthening monitoring, improving infrastructure, mindset issues of government departments, higher awareness, and incentivising good performance.

1

Introduction

The Government of India (GoI) and different state governments have been consistently endeavouring to reform public administration apparatus and its delivery of services to the citizens. The attempts are oriented towards providing better services—timely, hassle-free, convenient, and accessible. A number of committees and commissions have been set up by the GoI and state governments from time to time to study various aspects of reforming public administration as an institution and also its delivery mechanism.

One of the landmark initiatives in the saga of Indian governance reforms has been the Conference of Chief Ministers held in 1997 at New Delhi under the chairmanship of the Prime Minister. The Conference echoed the view that there is an urgent need for effecting changes in the system for better service delivery to the citizens. Accordingly, an Action Plan towards establishing an effective and responsive administration at the central and state levels was put forth during the Conference. The Action Plan focused on the need to take immediate corrective steps to restore faith of the people in the fairness, integrity, and responsiveness of public administration. This was the first time ever that they were certain strategies discussed for streamlining administration and improving pro-poor services.

The focus increased with the 10th Five Year Plan (2002-2007) highlighting the issues of governance like lack of sensitivity, transparency and accountability in many facets of the government service delivery (particularly those that have an interface with the public), and lack of credibility—the gap between the intent and the implementation—of some institutions in society. The Plan emphasised that the governance reform is critical for effective plan formulation and implementation to address the above problems. The 11th Five Year Plan (2007-2012) felt the need for a strong citizen-centric governance which could be attained by simplifying processes and services.

Citizen-centric public systems refer to those systems which deliver certain goods or services that are of utmost importance to citizens by using those tools and techniques which place citizens at the core of the entire public service delivery system. The activities of citizen-centric public systems are woven around the needs of the citizens, which facilitate them to lead a decent living by accessing better and qualitative services from time to time. Although the term decent living itself is difficult to define, yet there are certain elements which are equated with citizen-centric public systems and they are—simple, measurable, accountable, responsive and timeliness (SMART).

Every public system should have simple processes through which they can deliver the goods and services in the most effective and efficient manner. The government needs to focus on measurability of its services which in turn enables it to provide better and qualitative services. The term accountable refers to the activities wherein the focus is making the government agencies responsible for the delivery of services as per the standards prescribed in the Citizen Charters and any deviation from the Charters is considered an anathema from both the sides. A public system should be responsive to the needs of the citizens and serve the society at large, and the responsiveness is not a onetime affair but continuous focus for most of the democratic governments. Another important element of citizen-centric public system is transparency of its activities, which should transcend to the administrative system as well and finally the service delivery mechanism needs to be more in tune with the time frames so that the citizens receive timely services.

A good citizen-centric public system constantly strives towards improving delivery system so that services are delivered to the citizens to utmost satisfaction and moves in the direction of efficient delivery of services. The administrative processes as well as the delivery systems are made efficient and effective to serve the final objective of citizen satisfaction and it is the responsibility of the governments to serve citizens in the best possible manner.

In this context, the role of IT (information technology) has come handy for the governments all over the world as IT has enabled the integration of back end and front end operations in the most effective and efficient manner. The integration has led to better service delivery to the citizens so that they receive timely and transparent services from the government agencies, and the whole of gamut of such governance is termed as e-governance.

The Government of Andhra Pradesh (GoAP) was one of the states that took early initiatives to reform governance with the help of technology-enabled processes. The government came out with a governance reforms and public management strategy with a commitment to transform governance and provide a citizen-centric, clean, genuine and caring government. The strategy focussed on commitment, accountability, responsiveness and inclusiveness of the governance systems. The approach of GoAP aimed at establishing an accountable and transparent public administration system which could ensure effective service delivery to the citizens, both rural and urban.

Against such a back ground, the book focuses on how the GoAP has focussed on various initiatives culminating in the single point contact for accessing different government services from one point shop. The citizens who had to knock the doors of different departments without much fruitful results are now able to access the government services in a faster and reliable manner. The GoAP has taken some initiatives towards fostering citizen-centric public systems which over a period of time resulted in Mee Seva which aims to provide various services to the citizens by a click of a mouse.

Some of the initiatives taken by the GoAP are discussed below.

Identifying Focus Departments

The government departments with high public interface, which include health, education, social welfare, rural development, revenue, police, etc., were identified for streamlining service delivery. Issues and problems faced by the citizens in accessing information, services and other benefits from these departments were identified. Special teams—Strategy & Performance Innovation Units (SPIUs)—were set up to play a key role in facilitating the process of change required for heralding governance reforms in the concerned departments in specific and across the government in general.

People at the Centre of Service Delivery

The focus of the GoAP was to facilitate the establishment of citizen-centric service delivery model over a period of time. Numerous models were designed and implemented towards the objective of placing the citizens in the centre of the service delivery model. Some of those ideas include the following:

- Identification of citizen service needs and expectations based on citizen surveys and taking citizen priorities into account (user need analysis).
- People as customers rather than beneficiaries; trust in the efficacy of collaborating with citizens and taking measures to build trust among citizens.
- Create single window cells for one-stop user-friendly service delivery, reducing waiting time and providing service within assured time frame, e.g. e-Seva centres, Mee Seva centres etc.
- Ensure timely and quality services to citizens by adopting thorough benchmarking practices.
- Involve people in the design, delivery, assessment and redesign of public services through mechanisms such as consultation, focus groups, feedback mechanisms, social audit, people's audit, participatory appraisal and other such practices.
- Develop user feedback mechanisms such as Citizen's Report Card surveys to plan and implement services in a better way.
- Create public awareness about the services provided by each agency of the government with all the information required by the user.
- Provide transparency in administrative systems for accountability.
- Considering constitution of citizens' advisory boards, citizens' councils, citizens' committees in departments.
- Encourage SHGs (self-help groups), NGOs (non-government organisations), CBOs (community based organisations), consumer organisations and civil society groups by facilitating skill development for effective participation in governance.

- Provide people with easy access to government offices and public servants.

Citizen Charters and Service Charters

Providing time-bound services has been one of the hallmarks of a good governance system and the GoAP has been in the forefront in the preparation, implementation, monitoring, and evaluation of Citizen Charters covering the following areas:

- Consultation: people should be consulted regarding service levels and quality.
- Service Standards: people must be made aware of what to expect in terms of level or quantity and quality of services.
- Access: people should have equal access to the services to which they are entitled.
- Courtesy: people should be treated with courtesy and consideration.
- Information: people must receive full and accurate information about their services.
- Openness and Transparency: people should be informed about government departments' operations, budget, and management structures.
- Redress: people are entitled to an explanation and remedial action if the promised standard of service is not delivered.
- Value for money: public services should be provided economically and efficiently.

The GoAP proposed that departments formulate and implement Citizen Charters and the existing Citizen Charters in departments would be evaluated from time to time.

Redressal of Public Grievances

The GoAP also came out with the idea of machinery for the redressal of public grievances, and one proposal was the computerised and internet based Public Grievances Redressal Monitoring System (PGRMS). It was to be developed to help citizens to lodge complaints and monitor the progress of action thereon on their grievances over the internet. An independent institutional framework was supposed to oversee the action on redressal of public grievances. Some of the initiatives taken up as part of strengthening the redressal mechanism include the following:

- Establishment of an institutional mechanism to independently oversee redressal of public grievances by government agencies.
- Strengthening of consumer courts.
- Clarification of grievances redressal machinery under citizen charters.
- Establishment of call centres and development of web-enabled grievance/call monitoring systems.
- Involvement of the civil society in processing and tracking disposal of grievances.
- Fixing timeframes for grievance redressal and penal actions, if grievances are not addressed.
- Periodical monitoring of grievance redressal at the 'head of the department' and 'chief secretary' levels using computerised monitoring system.

Reducing Citizen's Interface with Government Departments

Corruption and inconvenience to the citizens can be reduced to a great extent by reducing citizens' interface with government departments. In this regard the following initiatives were considered by the GoAP:

- Cutting down of personal/physical interface between the citizens and the government agencies.
- Single-window stations, such as the customer service centres or electronic service counter like e-Seva as one-stop shops, preferably manned by private sector agencies on the basis of performance contracts.
- Payment of all government dues through banks, online modes, or specially organised transparent counters.

Anti-Corruption Strategy

As corruption paralyses the efforts of the government to provide basic services to the citizens, the GoAP took certain steps to combat corruption in the process of reforming governance, and they include:

- Strengthened preventive vigilance measures for combating corruption at various levels.
- Spreading awareness among citizens and involved civil society groups in formulating the agenda.
- Delegating authority and resources to units below the state government like local bodies and executive agencies with open covenants governing the use of delegated powers.
- Identifying corruption prone processes in each department and plugging the gaps through the use of technology.
- Monitoring court litigations involving corruption cases on fast track mode, and using information technology to fasten the process so that justice was rendered.
- Constitution of citizen committees in key departments to guide the agencies in the implementation of anti-corruption measures.
- Interface between the public and government offices may be minimised through the use of information technology and creation of public service counters.

ICT Initiatives in Andhra Pradesh

Information and communication technologies (ICT) can enable the improvement and innovation necessary for providing affordable and accessible services. This apart, ICT can be used to revamp and refurbish the processes of governance. However for that, a massive improvement of connectivity through broadband services is required. The endeavours of the GoAP have resulted in the establishment of citizen-centric public systems equipped to deliver services to the citizens with utmost ease and simplicity. This has been possible as the application of technology in government offices has graduated in the following manner:

- Computerisation: efforts limited to digitisation of records for the convenience of government officials, enabling them to take quick decisions.
- Information: the focus has been on enabling the citizens to access the information from the government departments with the help of Internet.
- Payments: this phase provided an opportunity to the citizens to pay their utility bills in a hassle-free manner. Citizens started feeling better about the service delivery mechanism.
- Services: the acclimatisation of citizens to a single contact point for the payment of utility bills has helped the government to bring multiple services being rendered by different departments under one roof.

With all such efforts proving to be highly convenient for the citizens, the GoAP has taken the citizen services a step ahead. The frequently availed services have been put together as an integrated citizen service model called Mee Seva. Mee Seva is a gateway which offers citizens technology-based single point services in an easier and faster manner with minimum or no personal/physical interface between the citizens and the government agencies.

2

Mee Seva Project

The National e-Governance Plan (NeGP) formulated by the Government of India (GoI), visualised that all basic services availed by citizens will be delivered in an easier and faster manner. The Plan provided an overarching framework for e-Governance initiatives in the country by bringing in convergence among various initiatives across departments and maximising benefits to the citizens. Based on these ideas, massive initiatives have been taken across the country to build basic infrastructure which helps in services reaching the remotest villages, computerisation of records in key service delivery departments, accessibility of the internet, establishment of kiosks among other things. The vision statement of NeGP state that the ultimate objective is to bring public services closer to the citizens. The institutional mechanism suggested by the government for implementation of this plan is setting up of service delivery points called Common Service Centres (CSCs): it can have interface with the citizens and provide services to them conveniently.

Before Mee Seva started, government service delivery systems were manual and opaque. Citizens recalled difficulties in accessing government offices mired in tedious office processes and longer time lags in service delivery. Scenes of overcrowded government offices with unfriendly employees combined with chronic absenteeism, inefficiency in service delivery, long queues, resultant delays and rent-seeking were common. In addition, the focus in administration was more on following procedures and keeping records than catering to the needs of citizens, thus losing the vision and treating citizens as the subject rather than the object of development.

The power of ICT (information, communication and technology) was primarily underutilised and most of the departments had ineffective interfaces for service delivery. Government employees too, were not satisfied as the system induced drudgery; and lack of occupational motivation was affecting overall productivity.

Meanwhile, the ICT infrastructure in Andhra Pradesh (AP) was growing at a brisk pace. Information technology is generally considered as an indispensable instrument for rejuvenating existing government service delivery mechanism to provide good governance. The Government of Andhra Pradesh (GoAP) had initiated e-Seva in 2001 with the intention to provide convenience to citizens incorporating ICT-driven systematic changes in government procedures. e-Seva was started to provide bill payment services for various government departments and private organisations in urban parts of the state. Though e-Seva succeeded in reducing the drudgery of bill-payments, it was still serving like a 'post-office': accepting applications, sending them by post to the concerned office, receiving them, and then handing them over to the citizens without functioning as an integrated service delivery model.

Subsequently CSCs were established to extend similar benefits to the rural citizens of the state as part of the NeGP. But lack of services roll out and general apathy of the departments made them completely unviable and hardly anybody survived. The infrastructure created under NeGP like AP State Data Centre (SDC), State Wide Area Network (SWAN) was also grossly underutilised.

The process of metamorphosis of e-Seva to Mee Seva started against this backdrop. The idea was to make use of the infrastructure already created and push various departments to align with such thinking. The selection of departments depended on the extent of citizen-centricity of such departments. The focus of e-Governance was tweaked to identify the services and set in motion business process re-engineering to support such service delivery. Mee Seva was brought in to bring in true convergence of all the NeGP initiatives for rendering G2C (government-to-citizen) services in a transparent, fast and secure way.

Government initiated work on providing a reliable and secured architecture for delivering various citizen services with data securely hosted in the SDC, to be used by each of the state designated agencies providing services through CSCs.

Mee Seva is a G2C/G2B (government-to-business) service delivery platform for faster, easier, and transparent delivery of services to the citizens. It entails central pooling of all the records, issuance of digital signatures of the officers concerned, and facilitating interface through CSCs. People's documents such as certificates, permits etc., are issued by the government through kiosks in this system. The best part of Mee Seva is that the documents provided are digitally signed and electronically verifiable. Figure 2.1 illustrates how Mee Seva is designed to be effective.

Figure 2.1

Mee Seva at the Heart of e-Governance

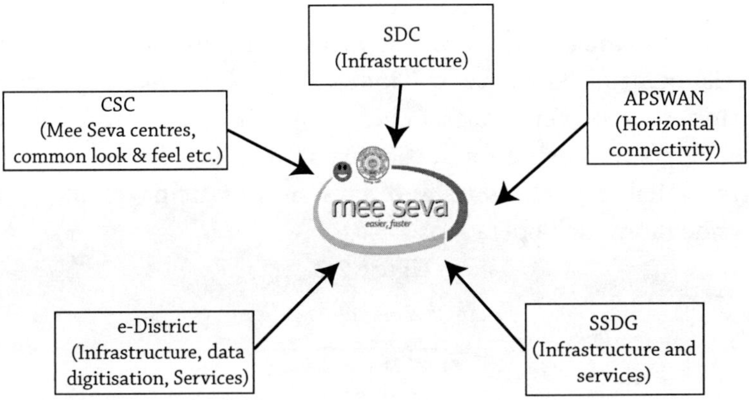

In Mee Seva, the personal/physical interface between the government departments and the citizens is eliminated as the requests collected from citizens at Mee Seva centres are scanned and sent to the designated officer. At the prescribed time, citizens can collect the certificates at Mee Seva centres rather than visit the concerned government department. The system has a specific timeframe for the delivery of each service and thus, the clearance of citizen requests can be monitored from time to time. The timeframe for each service is given in the Citizen Charters affixed at each of the Mee Seva centres all over the state of Andhra Pradesh and the entire IT architecture pertaining to Mee Seva is well designed and well integrated with the kiosks and government departments as shown in Figure 2.2.

Mee Seva has taken the citizens on board as it helped them to transact with the government departments using IT (information technology) in the most hassle-free manner. The government departments with which the citizens perform a large number of transactions have been reengineered and IT has been added as a tool for better service delivery. Departments like revenue, registration, etc., have been consulted and insights were developed before initiating the entire programme.

Once the programme was initiated, delivery channels and kiosks were established across the state, both in rural and urban areas. To serve these channels and kiosks, a robust IT mechanism was developed along with back end operations—digitisation of records, creation of databases for social services, centralisation of databases, establishment of hardware, collaboration with service departments, creation of e-Governance society, capacity building of various stakeholders, provision for stationary items, establishment of a call centre available at all hours and days, automatic payment gateway, alongside more such operations.

Figure 2.2

IT Architecture of Mee Seva

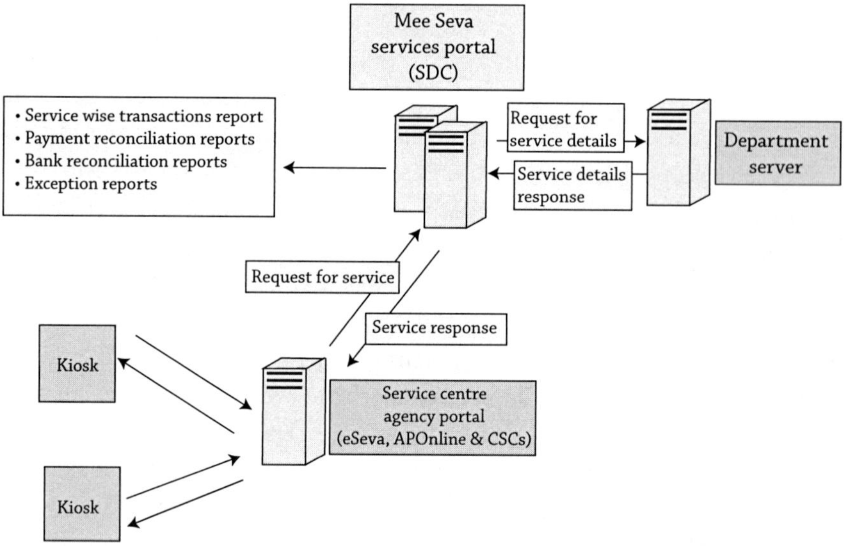

All such activities were coordinated to ensure that the citizens receive these services without going multiple times to multiple places and points. This made the life of citizens better as they received government services at a single point without any hardship. To ensure that Mee Seva sustains without much dependence on government, it has been decided to launch the same system on a PPP (public private partnership) mode where Mee Seva centres are run by authorised agents who in turn are appointed by authorised service providers. The PPP mode entails the collection of user charges to provide better and quality services.

The impact of Mee Seva can be gauged from more than 50,000 transactions that are being done per day. The speed with which the services are being provided to the citizens should not just inspire but also be replicated in other states. For example, under Mee Seva citizens are availing certain services within 15 minutes whereas in the earlier system the same service was availed by the citizens in 2-5 days. With more services in the offing, Mee Seva is expected to be a trailblazer in providing better and quality services to the citizens of AP.

Mee Seva symbolises process reengineering in government yielding innumerable benefits—innovation, accountability, cost effectiveness, user friendly, citizen-centric, number of services offered, geographical coverage, efficient utilisation of resources, streamlining the back-end processes, e-inclusion, sustainability and above all, the convenience of availing services in a timely fashion without extra costs.

Mee Seva by ending the 'tyranny of ink signatures' has heralded a silent but gigantic revolution which has swept away the archaic processes and has facilitated the establishment of a truly citizen-centric governance system.

However, a lot of preparatory work was done prior to the launch of this project. One of the major steps prior to launching the Mee Seva project was that the government brought out Andhra Pradesh Information Technology (Electronic Service Delivery, ESD) Rules, 2011 vide G.O.Ms.10, IT&C Department, dated 18.10.2011. The key features of Mee Seva are as follows:

- Use of digital certificates: The ESD Rules 2011 provides for enabling and regulating the filing of forms of applications, and for the issue/grant of digitally signed licenses, permits, certificates, sanctions or approvals and the receipt of payment for the delivery of services electronically to the users.

- Delivery of services through electronic mode: The government departments are directed to publish within 180 days the various services they would provide through electronic mode, the timelines within which it would be done, and the service standards to conform to. It also directs the departments to identify nodal officers responsible for the above initiatives. The maximum timeline granted for departments to switch over to the electronic mode of service delivery is within next five years.
- Institutional mechanism for delivery: The Director, EDS,[1] (e-Seva) has been designated Director of ESD as per the Act to oversee the entire operations of electronic service delivery by departments. Authorising service providers, ensuring accountable and efficient service delivery and entire responsibility of supervision has been vested with the Director.

  At the District level, a Special Deputy Collector (SDC) has been designated to ensure smooth implementation, better coordination and review with the participating departments like the concerned revenue authorities, municipalities, offices of electricity distribution companies and any other department whose services are being offered through Mee Seva. The district heads are also responsible for ensuring readiness of departmental databases, digitally signing them, and installing the requisite hardware and software. The other major responsibility of SDCs is the redressal of customer grievances and smooth functioning of services.

  Each district has been provided with one resource person reporting to the Joint Collector/Additional Director, ESD to provide support to the concerned officers in the district. The centres delivering Mee Seva services have been advised by the state government to

1. Electronically deliverable services.

have a common look across the state including things like colour scheme, display boards, notice boards, etc.

- Implementation aspect: The ICT Department, the nodal agency in the implementation of the project held consultative meetings with supply side stakeholders from Revenue Department, Registration Department, district heads, technical support organisations like National Informatics Centres (NIC), AP Online and others.

  The salient feature of this project is that there is a centralised database which ensures uniformity, data security, integrity and reliability. This data can be accessed by various stakeholders through the SWAN. The other key feature is that of digital signatures. Manual methods have been completely kept aside in the implementation of this project.

  As a part of the plan, the Service Delivery Points are supposed to have a standardised look with display boards, posters, common facilities, and other amenities. Responsibility for monitoring the field operations has been given to the service centre agency.

Services Included

The project works on an integrated service delivery model to provide a single entry point for a wide range of services to the citizens in a 'easier and faster' manner. The project provides different types of services for departments like Revenue, Registration, etc. The services offered by Mee Seva have been categorised into Category A and Category B. The distinction is based on certain parameters which are elaborated upon as below.

Category A

- These are the services to be given across the counter by the kiosk operator.
- No supporting documents required to be given at the kiosk.

The procedure for processing requests under Category A services has been outlined by the government in the department user manual:

- All the digitally signed departmental databases stored in the SDC.
- Citizen comes to CSC for submission of application of certificates.
- Applicant purchases and fills up a physical application form.
- CSC operator enters the details online, accesses database, pulls the relevant record, and issues the digitally signed paper.
- A receipt of acknowledgement is also given to the applicant.

Category B

- These services are statutory in nature and require notices/hearings/field inspections.
- The time required for delivery of services is prescribed in 'service level agreements' as per the existing rule positions.
- Citizens come to CSC and submit application form for availing required certificate and pay the charges.
- The operator enters the details in the online application software and issues a receipt to the applicant.
- Citizen applications received at the Mee Seva centres are electronically transferred to the concerned departmental official.
- The concerned official logs into the online portal and downloads the application, verifies the records, approves/rejects the citizen application as per existing government procedures.
- The certificates are printed and despatched to the applicants address or delivered through kiosks.
- All the certificates issued through Mee Seva are generated using secured stationery with eight security features to make duplication difficult.

All the digitally signed certificates are kept stored in the State Electronic Certificate Repository (SECR). The kiosk takes printouts that are delivered on the applicant's address, and details of delivery are sent by SMS to the applicant.

In case the application is rejected, *tahsildar* has to enter the reasons for rejection. As indicated in the Mee Seva portal, the total number of requests received through Mee Seva till November 2012 were as follows:

Total requests :	66,72,755
Category A :	22,36,293
Category B :	44,36,462
Total approved :	38,51,237
Total rejected :	2,48,401
Pending within Service Level Agreements (SLA):	3,02,215
Pending beyond SLA:	34,606

The increasing expectations of the citizens due to the integration of the technology and the widespread usage of web applications have led the government to initiate changes in its delivery processes. The GoI took lead in this regard and provided the necessary infrastructure for the state governments for providing e-services to the citizens. However, providing e-services to the citizens necessitate a new model of public service delivery which entails massive business process engineering at the department level, integration of the data banks across the departments and the front end kiosks, fool proof security of data, authentication and up gradation of records from time to time and, timely and transparent services to the citizens.

The way Mee Seva has percolated across the state of Andhra Pradesh is an indication of the fact that the efforts of the GoI to make the public services delivery simple and fast has led to fruitful results. Of course, the GoAP too has exhibited its willingness to opt for new ways of service delivery to the citizens under a single roof as per the standards of the Citizen Charters. The indications are clear about the successful implanting of Mee Seva as a service provider of the government services in the most transparent and accountable manner.

3

Project Scope and Methodology

The Mee Seva project has been operational from 2011 and it was intended to evaluate the service delivery aspects by carrying out an impact assessment study. The focus was to be on the service delivery with reference to its implementation as well as customer satisfaction. The evaluation study was taken up by Institute of Public Enterprise, Hyderabad[1] with the following objectives:

- To study the overall functioning of Mee Seva.
- To study the citizen/user satisfaction with Mee Seva services.
- To analyse the issues/problems faced by citizens.

For the purpose of the study, the key stakeholders identified include:

- Customers/Citizens/Users.
- Departments involved in the Mee Seva portal.
- Delivery channels: kiosk owners and operators.
- Service Centre Agencies (SCAs): AP Online, Spanco etc.

Research Approach

The survey had the following research approach:

- Towards the objective of evaluating Mee Seva, a survey was undertaken to take feedback from the customers of Mee Seva and know their satisfaction level.
- The operational difficulties faced by the CSC operators were elicited with the help of a structured format.
- The departmental constraints, including coordination issues, mindset issues etc., were discussed with officials at various levels with the help of in-depth interviews.

1. Vide Lr.No.101/Mee Seva-evaluation/IT&C/Portal/2012 Dated: 5-10-2012

- Observation: general functioning of the system, the processes, the working procedures, etc., was also carried out by the field teams.

Services Covered

Mee Seva was started with an objective of providing a wide range of G2C (government to citizen) services. When the study was undertaken, there were 38 G2C services offered by Mee Seva, the categorisation of those services is:

Category A Services that are offered across the counter: 11.

Category B Services which are offered after a stipulated time: 27.

Table 3.1

Classification of Mee Seva Services

Type of Service	*Details of the Services Covered*
Category A	*Services at State Level*
	• Current Adangal
	• ISES-Income Certificate
	• ISES-Integrated Certificate
	• ISES-Residence Certificate
	• Duplicate Certificate Copy: Income
	• Duplicate Certificate Copy: Integrated
	• Duplicate Certificate Copy: Residence
	• Certified Copy of Registration
	• FMB Copy
	Exclusive GHMC Services
	• GHMC-Birth Certificate
	• GHMC-Death Certificate
Category B	*Services at State Level*
	• Income Certificate
	• Integrated Certificate
	• Residence Certificate
	• OBC Certificate
	• ROR-1B

contd...

...contd...

	• EBC Certificate • Family Member Certificate • Encumbrance Certificate • Mutation • Agriculture Income Certificate • Correction in Adangal/Pahani • No Earning Certificate • F-LINE Petition • Sub-division *Patta* • Village Map Copy *Services Recently Introduced at State Level* • Hospital Registration • Money Lending Licence Certificate • NFBS Certificate • No Objection Certificate • Pawn Broker Licence Certificate • School Registration • Apadhbandu Scheme *Exclusive GHMC Services* • GHMC: Child Name Inclusion • GHMC: Corrections in Birth Certificate • GHMC: Corrections in Death Certificate • GHMC: Non-Availability of Birth Certificate • GHMC: Non-Availability of Death Certificate

Note: ISES: Integrated Socio Economic Survey for Students; FMB: Field Measurement Book; GHMC: Greater Hyderabad Municipal Corporation; OBC: Other Backward Classes; ROR1B: Record of Right Form 1B; EBC: Economically Backward Class; NFBS: National Family Benefit Scheme.

Coverage

All the 23 districts in Andhra Pradesh (AP) were covered as a part of the study. The satisfaction levels of users/customers with respect to all the 38 services under Category A and B were covered.

In all, 1,370 Common Service Centre (CSC) operators were contacted to get the feedback about the functioning of Mee Seva.

Thirty (30) officials (Special Deputy Collectors, *Tahsildars*, VROs [Village Revenue Officers], Revenue Inspectors, District Registrars, officials in the IG Registrations and Stamps Department) were interviewed to unravel departmental issues and challenges.

Customer Satisfaction Survey

A total of 10,576 users/customers from both urban and rural areas (Mee Seva and kiosks) were contacted for feedback to get primary information on customer satisfaction related to Mee Seva services; 2,335 users/customers were contacted in person (100 users per district) and the rest 8,241 were contacted through telephone.

The purpose of meeting the citizens in person was to get a firsthand account of their satisfaction. The project team was interested in getting customer feedback at the very instant the service was provided. A sufficient proportion of the total sample of 10,576 i.e., 2,335 was taken from personal/field interviews. To have a feel of the

Table 3.2

Name of the Service and its Type

S No	*Name of the Service*	*Transactions in September*	*Type of Service*
1	Current Adangal	638696	High Volume
2	Income Certificate	448932	High Volume
3	Integrated Certificate	327038	High Volume
4	Residence Certificate	179715	High Volume
5	OBC Certificate	48703	High Volume
6	ROR-1B	36609	High Volume
7	EBC Certificate	15834	Medium Volume
8	ISES-Income Certificate	15324	Medium Volume
9	ISES-Integrated Certificate	13821	Medium Volume
10	Family Member Certificate	9214	Medium Volume
11	FMB Certificate	8870	Medium Volume
12	Mutation	8081	Medium Volume
13	ISES Services-Residence Certificate	3138	Medium Volume
14	Agriculture Income Certificate	870	Low Volume
15	Duplicate Certificate copy-Income	452	Low Volume
16	Duplicate Certificate copy-Integrated	296	Low Volume
17	Duplicate Certificate copy-Residence	293	Low Volume
18	No Earning Certificate	283	Low Volume
19	Corrections in Adangal	272	Low Volume

customer satisfaction from the urban and rural parts of each district, 50 users from urban area and 50 from rural area were selected from each district, covering at least two centres from urban and two centres from rural areas.

The 19 services offered by Mee Seva were categorised as high volume services, medium volume services and low volume services, based on the number of transactions taken place in the month of September 2012. If the number of transactions was above 30,000 then it was taken as high volume service. If it was between 3,000 to 30,000 transactions then it was considered as medium volume transactions, and if below 3,000 transactions then it was considered as low volume services.

The 8,241 respondents were apportioned equally among 23 districts for telephonic survey. Thus, 344 respondents were chosen for telephonic survey from each district. The assumption was that the field data pertaining to 100 responses (where the researchers spoke to the citizens availing Mee Seva services) will be from high volume services—those services which have been availed by the citizens maximum number of times.

Thus, the total sample size for the 19 services both telephonic and field survey stands at 10,576 (8,241+2,335). When an effort was made to apportion the sample across the services availed by the citizens in proportion to the number of transactions done in the month of September, it was been found that there was very less sample for low and medium level services. Thus, 8,241 respondents were chosen for their feedback on high volume services. Out of which feedback from 2,335 respondents was obtained through field survey. The remaining respondents, feedback was collected through telephonic survey for high volume services. Roughly 246 respondents per district were contacted in relation to high volume services. About 70 respondents per district were chosen for customer feedback towards medium level services. Within each of the category, equal weightage was given for all services and in all districts.

The telephonic survey and field survey were conducted as per the methodology described above. The number of citizens contacted both in person and through telephone for each district is presented in Table 3.3.

Table 3.3

District-wise Respondents Contacted under Field and Telephonic Survey

		Number of Citizens contacted	
S.No	*Name of the District*	*Field Survey*	*Telephonic Survey*
1	Adilabad	100	332
2	Anantapur	99	348
3	Chittoor	100	327
4	Cuddapah	100	396
5	East Godavari	102	321
6	Guntur	97	341
7	Hyderabad	100	312
8	Karimnagar	100	350
9	Khammam	107	340
10	Krishna	100	345
11	Kurnool	100	361
12	Mahbubnagar	124	339
13	Medak	100	340
14	Nalgonda	98	334
15	Nellore	73	379
16	Nizamabad	103	354
17	Prakasam	85	335
18	Rangareddy	100	332
19	Srikakulam	100	357
20	Visakhapatnam	101	353
21	Vizianagaram	100	320
22	Warangal	100	345
23	West Godavari	102	338
	Total	2291	7899

Note: The figure includes the respondents contacted for high, medium, and low volume services (19 services).

A total of 14 services, of which 7 belonged exclusively to GHMC and the other 7 being services recently introduced at the state level, were studied by taking 30 respondents for each service. The customer satisfaction for these services was drawn through telephonic survey. The number of users contacted for a particular service was in some cases less than 30 due to non-availability of sufficient number of phone numbers, no response from user, or change in phone numbers.

The five services namely Encumbrance Certificate, certified copy of registration, F-Line Petition, sub-division data, village map were studied by taking 30 respondents per service as the number 30 was considered to be a sufficient size of sample to infer something. In other words, 150 respondents were contacted to get feedback about these services. The telephonic data provided mostly belonged to Chittoor district and in one or two cases to other districts.

For ready reference, the service names, number of users contacted and number of people contacted through telephones are given in Table 3.4.

Table 3.4

GHMC Services Respondents Contacted through Telephonic Survey

S.No	*Service Name*	*Telephone Nos Provided*	*Users Contacted*
GHMC Services			
1	Death Certificate	80	30
2	GHMC-Corrections In Birth Certificate	80	30
3	GHMC-Non-Availability of Birth Certificate	80	30
4	GHMC-Non-Availability of Death Certificate	21	10
5	GHMC-Corrections in Death Certificate	44	30
6	Birth Certificate	80	30
7	GHMC-Child Name Inclusion	80	30
Services recently introduced at State Level			
1	No Objection Certificate	80	30
2	NFBS Certificate	80	30
3	School Registration	52	30
4	Hospital Registration	32	21
5	Apathbandhu Scheme	18	14
6	Pawn Broker License Certificate	14	14
7	Money Lending License Certificate	16	13
	Total		342

Field Planning

A team of two people was sent to each district and all the 23 districts were covered. A total of 46 people were assigned for faster data collection based on the pre-agreed formats.

Telephonic Planning

About 25 people were employed to conduct the telephonic survey to collect responses from 7,898 respondents covering the 19 services.

Another 4 people were employed to collect feedback from 492 respondents covering exclusive GHMC services, services extended to state level recently, and services like Encumbrance Certificate, certified copy of registration, F-Line Petition, sub-division data, and village map.

Data Collection

The primary data was collected from various stakeholders including the supply side and the demand side stakeholders to get their views on the efficacy of service delivery by Mee Seva.

Research Instruments

Structured and semi-structured questionnaires and formats were designed as per the stakeholder requirements. Most of the questions were closed-ended while a few questions were open ended.

- A generic questionnaire was developed to assess the satisfaction levels of the users/customers across both Category A and B services, and tested using field and telephonic surveys.
- A separate online questionnaire was developed and feedback was taken from the CSC operators.
- A separate open-ended questionnaire was developed for discussion with the participating departments.

Framework for Assessing Overall Satisfaction

A broad framework for assessing satisfaction with Mee Seva services was developed. It includes the user's and supplier's perspective.

- Customer service preparedness: supply side.
- The CSC operator's level of knowledge about the services.
- Timeliness and quality of response time to the queries from the user.
- Level of understanding of user's needs and expectations.
- Awareness generation, communication efforts from the supply side and the CSC owner.

Standards of Service Delivery

- Timeliness of service delivery.
- Service delivery quality.

Customer Satisfaction

- Level of customer satisfaction.
- Factors influencing the level of customer satisfaction.
- Follow-up with users/citizens.
- Knowledge of citizen needs and requirements.

Grievance Redressal Procedures

- Responsiveness of service provider.
- Timeliness of complaint resolution.
- Empathy of the customer servicing staff.
- Knowledge of customer servicing staff.

Scheme of the Book

- Introduction: Provides background of e-Governance in Andhra Pradesh.
- Mee Seva Project: An overview of Mee Seva services.
- Project Scope and Methodology: Gives an overview of project scope and methodology.
- Results and Discussions: Provides service-wise and district-wise analysis of MEE Sev services.

- Stakeholder Discussions: Gives insights into the discussions with the stakeholders of Mee Seva.
- Conclusion and Summing Up: Sums up the project.

The focus of the study was to collect data from a large sample of more than then thousand respondents across Andhra Pradesh. The overall objective of the study was to assess as to how the citizens perceive Mee Seva as a service provider of those services which were hitherto provided by the government departments. Some of the issues that were taken into consideration while designing the study were quality, standards, correctness, timeframe, responsiveness, accountability, grievance handling, etc.

4

Results and Discussions

Introduction

"Mee Seva" in Telugu means, "At your service", i.e. service to citizens. It is a good governance initiative that incorporates the vision of National eGov Plan "Public Services Closer to Home" and facilitates single entry portal for entire range of G2C & G2B services. The objective of Mee Seva is to provide smart, citizen-centric, ethical, efficient and effective governance facilitated by technology. The initiative involves universal and non-discriminatory delivery of all government services to citizens and businessmen of all strata, and improved efficiency, transparency and accountability for the government. The initiative features transformed government-citizen interface at all levels of administration along with a shared governance model.

Mee Seva is one of the pioneer service delivery mechanisms found in India where the services being provided by the government are placed under one roof called CSCs—Citizen Service Centres. The CSCs enable the citizens to avail various services—income certificate, birth certificate, residence certificate, caste certificate, etc., which are necessary for the citizens to avail other government benefits like scholarships, subsidies, etc.

In fact, Mee Seva has been at the forefront in the delivery of the services to the citizens and has ushered a new era in the government-citizen interface where the standards of services are strictly adhered to by the CSCs. The CSCs act like a third party and provide the necessary interface between the government departments and the citizens. The CSC operators are those individuals who are well versed with the nuances of the government services and are also aware of various procedures to be followed for enabling the citizens to avail better and timely services.

Mee Seva has led to transformation in the way public services are delivered to the citizens as a part of e-governance model of the

Government of India and is well supported by the state governments. The Government of Andhra Pradesh (GoAP) provided the necessary fillip for all those activities aimed at enhancing the standards of citizen services and one such gigantic step is Mee Seva. The Information Technology (IT) Department of GoAP acts as a nodal authority in regulating the affairs of Mee Seva and provides the necessary support in terms of IT facilities and necessary approvals for the integration of government agencies and their activities.

Given the increasing emphasis on good governance and further focus on 'maximum governance', Mee Seva is the right step in the right direction as the focus of good governance and maximum governance is citizen engagement through better delivery of services. It also found that the citizens who availed the services through Mee Seva have found the entire model of public service delivery more transparent and timely, which was missing earlier. Given further impetus and encouragement, Mee Seva is prone to become one of the leading service programme in sync with the good governance initiatives.

Overall Satisfaction of Mee Seva

Figure 4.1 shows that the number of respondents who expressed positive opinion towards Mee Seva is 63 per cent and the respondents who have expressed okay are 35 per cent. Only 2 per cent of the respondents have termed it as average. The inference that can be drawn from the figure is that satisfaction levels about Mee Seva services are high among the respondents.

Figure 4.1

State-wide Overall Satisfaction

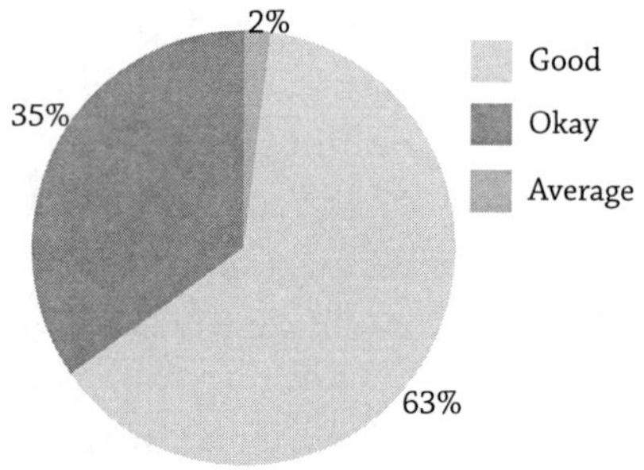

Figure 4.1(a) shows that the number of respondents who expressed positive opinion towards Category A services of Mee Seva is 64 per cent and the respondents who have expressed okay are 34 per cent. The inference that can be drawn from the figure is that the respondents are happy with Category A services being offered by Mee Seva.

Figure 4.1(b) shows that the number of respondents who expressed positive opinion towards Mee Seva is 63 per cent and the respondents who have expressed okay are 35 per cent The inference that can be drawn from the figure is that the respondents are happy with Category B services as well.

Figure 4.1(a)

State-wide Overall Satisfaction: Category A Services

Figure 4.1(b)

State-wide Overall Satisfaction: Category B Services

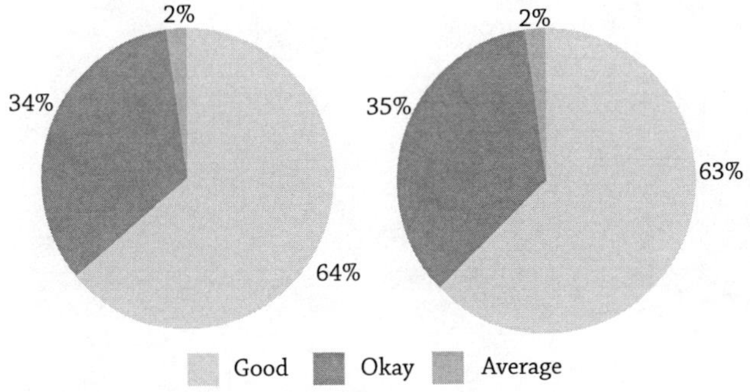

Overall Satisfaction of Services

The service-wise analysis shows that there are some services, such as OBC Caste Certificate, Current Adangal, Integrated Certificate, Income Certificate and ISES-Income Certificate, which have received accolades from citizens.

Service-wise Analysis

The satisfaction levels towards different services of Mee Seva were measured under three categories—good, okay and average. In each of the categories of classification, top three districts were identified based on the response to that category.

No.	*Name of the Service*	*Overall Satisfaction*
1.	OBC Caste Certificate	75.00%
2.	Current Adangal	67.50%
3.	Integrated Certificate	67.49%
4.	Income Certificate	65.69%
5.	ISES-Income Certificate	65.52%
6.	EBC Certificate	64.37%
7.	FMB COPY	63.35%
8.	Residence Certificate	62.38%
9.	ISES-Integrated Certificate	61.75%
10.	Mutation	59.93%
11.	Family Member Certificate	54.40%
12.	ROR-1B	48.64%

Table 4.1

District-wise Overall Satisfaction

District Name	*Satisfaction %*	*Average No. of Visits to Mee Seva Centre*	*Corruption %*
Visakhapatnam	92.51	2.51	1.10
Nalgonda	92.36	1.39	11.34
Mahbubnagar	89.20	1.28	0.65
Srikakulam	82.06	1.62	6.13
Nizamabad	80.44	2.44	4.39
Vizianagaram	79.76	1.80	4.52
Chittoor	77.75	2.75	4.68
Kurnool	77.66	2.39	6.07
Khammam	73.38	1.98	8.95
Prakasam	71.36	2.48	2.63
Anantapur	70.69	1.73	11.41
Cuddapah	69.72	2.24	12.40
East Godavari	64.29	2.27	10.00
Rangareddy	62.95	2.41	2.43
West Godavari	60.96	2.25	1.82
Adilabad	53.61	1.64	12.30
Hyderabad	42.98	2.19	11.66
Karimnagar	41.78	2.48	5.58
Medak	37.21	1.69	2.51
Krishna	34.91	2.50	10.34
Warangal	32.81	2.28	1.80
Guntur	32.42	2.61	11.19
Nellore	23.11	2.39	6.67

Current Adangal

The top districts under the good category are Visakhapatnam, Srikakulam and Nalgonda followed by Nellore, Medak and Krishna under the okay category.

Table 4.2

Service-wise Analysis: Current Adangal

Service Name	*Name of the District*	*Good (%)*	*Name of the District*	*Okay (%)*	*Name of the District*	*Average (%)*
	Visakhapatnam	100	Nellore	84	Rangareddy	11
Current Adangal	Srikakulam	95	Medak	72	East Godavari	9
	Nalgonda	95	Krishna	58	Vizianagaram	8

Note: Data was clubbed together for drawing some inferences for service-wise analysis for all services.

Analysis: The data indicates that in two districts, Nalgonda and Srikakulam, more than 90 per cent of the respondents rated overall usefulness/satisfaction with Mee Seva as good, while in Visakhapatnam, 100 per cent respondents agreed on the overall usefulness/satisfaction with Mee Seva. 70 to 80 per cent of the respondents from Adilabad, Cuddapah, Khammam, Kurnool, Prakasam, Rangareddy and Vizianagaram districts accepted the overall usefulness/satisfaction of Mee Seva. In districts like Guntur, Karimnagar and Krishna, more than 55 per cent termed it as okay. Similar views were expressed by 75 to 85 per cent of the respondents in Medak and Nellore districts.

The data indicates that in districts like Adilabad, Anantapur, Cuddapah, Mahbubnagar, Nalgonda, Medak, and Visakhapatnam the respondents have visited Mee Seva service centre only once to avail Current Adangal services. More than 50 per cent of the respondents have visited the centre only once which can be termed as highly satisfactory for the citizens.

All the respondents in districts like Mahbubnagar, Rangareddy, Visakhapatnam, Vizianagaram and Warangal stated that they did not pay any extra money for availing services from Mee Seva centre which is an accomplishment for institutions supported by the government. More than 80 per cent of the respondents in districts like Adilabad,

Anantapur, Chittor, Cuddapah, Guntur, Karimnagar, Khammam, Krishna, Kurnool, Medak, Nalgonda, Nellore, Nizamabad, Prakasam, Srikakulam and West Godavari, too have echoed similar opinion.

Income Certificate

The top districts in good category are Vizianagaram, Mahbubnagar and West Godavari followed by Nellore, Warangal and Hyderabad in okay category.

Table 4.3

Service-wise Analysis: Income Certificate

Service Name	*Name of the District*	*Good (%)*	*Name of the District*	*Okay (%)*
	Vizianagaram	93	Nellore	75
Income Certificate	Mahbubnagar	89	Warangal	67
	West Godavari	88	Hyderabad	64

Analysis: The data indicates that in seven districts—Mahbubnagar, Nalgonda, Nellore, Rangareddy, Visakhapatnam, Vizianagaram and West Godavari, more than 80 per cent of the respondents expressed the overall usefulness/satisfaction with Mee Seva services as good. Meanwhile, 60 to 80 per cent of the respondents from eight districts—Anantapur, Chittor, Cuddapah, East Godavari, Khammam, Kurnool, Prakasam and Srikakulam expressed the view that Mee Seva centres are useful for availing services. In four districts, Guntur, Karimnagar, Krishna and Medak, 50 to 55 per cent of the respondents expressed the level of satisfaction with Mee Seva centres as okay whereas the number is 75 per cent for Nellore. Except in Visakhapatnam, where the number of respondents who categorised Mee Seva as average is less than 10 per cent, and in many cases it is even less than 5 per cent.

The data indicates that more than 80 per cent of the respondents received services in the very first visit to Mee Seva centres and those districts are Mahbubnagar, Nalgonda and Medak, whereas in districts like Adilabad, Anantapur, Cuddapah and Vizianagarm, 60 to 70 per cent of the respondents agreed that they received services in the very first instance which is commendable.

Furthermore, the data indicates that in districts like Mahbubnagar, Visakhapatnam, Vizianagaram and West Godavari, all the respondents

(100%) stated that they did not pay any money to avail the services from Mee Seva, and in districts like Adilabad, Anantapur, Chittor, Cuddapah, East Godavari, Guntur, Karimnagar, Kurnool, Khammam, Medak, Nellore, Nizamabad, Prakasam, Rangareddy, Srikakulam and Warangal, more than 90 per cent of the respondents stated that they did not pay any extra money for availing services.

Integrated Certificate

The top districts in good category are Visakhapatnam, Mahbubnagar, Prakasam and Warangal. Rangareddy and Krishna districts are in the okay category.

Table 4.4

Service-wise Analysis: Integrated Certificate

Service Name	*Name of the District*	*Good (%)*	*Name of the District*	*Okay (%)*	*Name of the District*	*Average (%)*
Integrated Certificate	Visakhapatnam	100	Warangal	74	Cuddapah	4
	Mahbubnagar	93	Rangareddy	71	Nizamabad	4
	Prakasam	89	Krishna	65	Rangareddy	4

Analysis: The data indicates that in districts like Mahbubnagar, Nalgonda, Nizamabad, Prakasam, Visakhapatnam and Vizianagaram and West Godavari, 80 to 90 per cent of the respondents stated that Mee Seva is very useful in accessing different services. In the same vein, in districts like Anantapur, Cuddapah, East Godavari, Hyderabad, Khammam, Kurnool, Nellore and Srikakulam, 60 to 80 per cent of the respondents found Mee Seva useful. In districts like Warangal, Rangareddy and Krishna, 60 to 80 per cent of the respondents have found Mee Seva okay and all the districts, a negligible number of respondents which is less than 5 per cent have shown the performance of Mee Seva as average.

The data indicates that in districts like Karimnagar, Mahbubnagar, Medak, Nizamabad, Rangareddy, Visakhapatnam, Vizianagaram and West Godavari all the respondents stated that they did not pay any money for availing the services. In all the remaining districts—Adilabad, Anantapur, Chittor, Cuddapah, East Godavari, Guntur, Hyderabad, Karimnagar, Kurnool, Krishna, Nalgonda, Nellore, Prakasam, Srikakulam, and Warangal, 80 to 90 per cent of the respondents have stated that they did not pay any money for availing the services of Mee Seva. This is a tremendous accomplishment of Mee Seva where all the respondents (100%) from 8 districts out of 23 districts have stated that they did not pay extra money for availing the services.

Moreover, the data indicates that 80 to 90 per cent of the respondents from districts like Mahbubnagar, Srikakulam and West Godavari stated that they visited the Mee Seva centre only once to avail the services, and 60 to 80 per cent of the respondents from Adilabad, Anantapur, Khammam, Medak, Nalgonda, Rangareddy and Warangal, too expressed the same view. In some districts like Chittor, East Godavari, Guntur, Krishna, Kurnool, Nizamabad and Warangal, 40 to 60 per cent of the respondents stated that they went twice to receive services from the centres.

Residence Certificate

The top districts in good category are Mahbubnagar, Nalgonda and Vizianagaram. They are followed by Nellore, Medak and Karimnagar in okay category.

Table 4.5

Service-wise Analysis: Residence Certificate

Service Name	*Name of the District*	*Good (%)*	*Name of the District*	*Okay (%)*	*Name of the District*	*Average (%)*
Residence Certificate	Mahbubnagar	100	Nellore	75	Khammam	18
	Nalgonda	93	Medak	75	West Godavari	4
	Vizianagaram	92	Karimnagar	67	Nellore	4

Analysis: The data indicates that in the district of Mahbubnagar all the respondents categorised Mee Seva as useful and good. The same view is expressed by 90 per cent of the respondents in Nalgonda, Visakhapatnam and Vizianagaram. Similar view is expressed by 60 to 80 per cent of the respondents in the districts like Anantapur, Chittoor, Cuddapah, Kurnool, Prakasam, Nizamabad and Rangareddy. Between 60 to 80 per cent of the respondents expressed feeling okay towards Mee Seva in districts like Karimnagar, Krishna, Medak, Nellore and Warangal.

Further, the data indicates that in districts like Karimnagar, Mahbubnagar, Medak, Rangareddy, Srikakulam and Warangal, all the respondents stated that no extra money was given for availing the services. Similarly, 80 to 99 per cent of the respondents in districts like Adilabad, Anantapur, Chittoor, Cuddapah, East Godavari, Guntur, Hyderabad, Krishna, Kurnool, Nellore, Nizamabad, Prakasam, Visakhapatnam, Vizianagaram and West Godavari also expressed a similar view. In the district of Nalgonda, around 25 per cent of the respondents admitted that they have paid more money than what is required. In the district of Khammam, 20 per cent of the respondents admitted to doing so.

The data indicates that in Nalgonda and Srikakulam, 90 to 100 per cent of the respondents have visited Mee Seva centre only once for availing the services. The same opinion is expressed by 70 to 80 per cent of the respondents in districts like Hyderabad, Khammam, and Nellore.

OBC Certificate

The top districts in good category are Visakhapatnam, Mahbubnagar and Kurnool; followed by Nellore, Guntur and Krishna in okay category.

Table 4.6

Service-wise Analysis: OBC Certificate

Service Name	*Name of the District*	*Good (%)*	*Name of the District*	*Okay (%)*	*Name of the District*	*Average (%)*
OBC Certificate	Visakhapatnam	96	Nellore	92	Medak	12
	Mahbubnagar	95	Guntur	88	Guntur	5
	Kurnool	89	Krishna	70	Karimnagar	5

Analysis: The data indicates that 80 to 100 per cent have termed Mee Seva as good and useful. This response came from districts like Chittoor, Cuddapah, Khammam, Kurnool, Mahbubnagar, Nalgonda, Nizamabad, Rangareddy, Visakhapatnam, Vizianagaram and West Godavari. However, the same number of respondents termed Mee Seva as okay in the districts of Guntur and Nellore. Only in Medak district, response to Mee Seva was at average level.

The data also indicate that in districts like Chittoor, Mahbubnagar, Nizamabad, Prakasam, Rangareddy, Vishakhapatnam and West Godavari, all the respondents stated that they have not paid any extra money for availing the services. And the same view is echoed by 80 to 99 per cent of the respondents in Adilabad, Anantapur, Cuddapah, East Godavari, Hyderabad, Karimnagar, Khammam, Krishna, Kurnool, Medak, Nalgonda, Nellore, Srikakulam, Vizianagaram and Warangal. Only in the district of Guntur, more than 20 per cent of the respondents have stated that they paid extra money for availing the services, otherwise none of the respondents paid extra money in certain districts.

The data indicates that in the district of Mahbubnagar, all the respondents stated that they visited Mee Seva only once to avail the services and the same was expressed by more than 80 per cent of the respondents in the districts like Adilabad, Anantapur and Nalgonda. Between 40 to 60 per cent of the respondents in districts like Chittoor, Cuddapah, Hyderabad, Karimnagar, Krishna, Khammam, Prakasam, and Rangareddy, stated that they went twice to Mee Seva centre to avail the services.

ROR 1B

The top districts in good category are Nalgonda, Srikakulam and Kurnool followed by Hyderabad, Guntur and Warangal in okay category.

Table 4.7

Service-wise Analysis: ROR 1 B

Service Name	*Name of the District*	*Good (%)*	*Name of the District*	*Okay (%)*	*Name of the District*	*Average (%)*
	Nalgonda	100	Hyderabad	100	Krishna	16
ROR 1 B	Srikakulam	100	Guntur	93	West Godavari	10
	Kurnool	90	Warangal	91	Adilabad	6

Analysis: The data indicates that in the districts like Nalgonda and Srikakulam, all the respondents termed it as good and useful whereas all the respondents in the district of Hyderabad termed it as okay. Between 60 to 90 per cent of the respondents in districts like Chittoor, Cuddapah, Khammam, Mahbubnagar, Nizamabad, Prakasam, Visakhapatnam and Vizianagaram termed it as good and useful. Between 80 to 99 per cent of the respondents in districts like Guntur, Medak, Rangareddy, Warangal, and West Godavari stated that the Mee Seva service is okay.

The data also indicate that all the respondents (100%) in the districts like Guntur, Hyderabad, Kurnool, Medak, Nellore, Nizamabad, Srikakulam and Warangal have stated that they did not paid any extra money for availing the services. And similar views are expressed by 80 to 99 per cent of the respondents in the districts like Adilabad, Chittoor, Cuddapah, East Godavari, Karimnagar, Khammam, Krishna, Mahbubnagar, Nalgonda, Prakasam, Rangareddy, Visakhapatnam, Vizianagaram and West Godavari.

The data indicates that 80 to 90 per cent of the respondents stated that they visited Mee Seva centres only once in the districts of Mahbubnagar, Medak and Rangareddy. The same view is expressed by 60 to 80 per cent of the respondents in districts like Adilabad, Hyderabad, Khammam and Nalgonda. All the respondents of the East Godavari district stated that they visited twice and similar views were expressed by a little less than 80 per cent of the respondents in the districts Kurnool and Warangal. In the district of Nizamabad, less than 80 per cent of the respondents expressed that they have visited Mee Seva centre thrice.

EBC Certificate

The top districts in good category are Anantapur, East Godavari and Nalgonda followed by Guntur, Nellore and Warangal in okay category.

Table 4.8

Service-wise Analysis: EBC Certificate

Service Name	*Name of the District*	*Good (%)*	*Name of the District*	*Okay (%)*	*Name of the District*	*Average (%)*
	Anantapur	100	Guntur	100	Warangal	9
EBC Certificate	East Godavari	100	Nellore	100	Kurnool	8
	Nalgonda	100	Warangal	82	Medak	8

Analysis: The data indicates that 100 per cent of the respondents in districts like Anantapur, East Godavari, Nalgonda, Nizamabad, Srikakulam and Visakhapatnam have shown high satisfaction in availing the Mee Seva services. Similar views were expressed by 80 to 99 per cent of the respondents in districts like Chittoor, Khammam, Kurnool, Mahbubnagar and Prakasam and also 60 to 80 per cent of the respondents in the districts of Cuddapah, Hyderabad, Karimnagar, Vizianagaram and West Godavari have the same views; whereas 100 per cent of the respondents in districts of Guntur and Nellore expressed the Mee Seva services to be okay and just less than 10 per cent of the respondents expressed dissatisfaction with the services.

The data also indicate that all respondents in the districts of Karimnagar, Khammam, Mahbubnagar, Medak, Nalgonda, Nellore, Srikakulam, Prakasam, Visakhapatnam, Vizianagaram, Warangal, and West Godavari did not pay extra money for accessing physical forms and services. Only in the districts of Adilabad, Cuddapah and Rangareddy, did nearly 30 per cent of the respondents state that they paid more money than needed.

The data indicates that in the district of Srikakulam, just more than 90 per cent of the respondents stated that they went to Mee Seva centre only once to avail services and such an opinion was expressed by around 85 per cent of the respondents in Anantapur and Mahbubnagar. Between 30 to 40 per cent of respondents in the districts of Adilabad, Cuddapah, Guntur, Khammam, Nellore, Nizamabad, Rangareddy and Visakhampatnam expressed similar opinions. Coming to the district of East Godavari, 80 to 90 per cent of the respondents have stated that they went twice to avail the services and in the districts of Adilabad, Chittor, Guntur and Nalgonda, 60 to 70 per cent of the respondents have voiced same views.

ISES Income

The top districts in good category are East Godavari, Nalgonda and Srikakulam followed by Nellore, Guntur and Karimnagar in okay category.

Table 4.9

Service-wise Analysis: ISES Income

Service Name	*Name of the District*	*Good (%)*	*Name of the District*	*Okay (%)*	*Name of the District*	*Average (%)*
	East Godavari	100	Nellore	94	Adilabad	14
ISES Income	Nalgonda	100	Guntur	90	Visakhapatnam	10
	Srikakulam	100	Karimnagar	82	Khammam	9

Analysis: The data indicates that 80 to 100 per cent of the respondents in districts like Chittoor, Cuddapah, East Godavari, Khammam, Kurnool, Mahbubnagar, Nalgonda, Nizamabad, Srikakulam and Visakhapatnam expressed a high level of satisfaction. And similar views were expressed by 60 to 79 per cent of the respondents in the districts like Anantapur, Prakasam, Rangareddy, Vizianagaram, and West Godavari; whereas 50 to 70 per cent of the respondents in districts like Adilabad, Krishna, Medak and Warangal have expressed the Mee Seva services to be okay.

The data also indicate that 100 per cent of the respondents in districts like Adilabad, Chittoor, Guntur, Karimnagar, Mahbubnagar, Medak, Nalgonda, Nizamabad, Prakasa, Rangareddy, Srikakulam, Visakapatnam, Warangal and West Godavari did not paid any extra money for availing the Mee Seva services and similar view is expressed by 80 to 99 per cent of the respondents in districts like Anantapur, East Godavari, Khammam, Krishna, Nellore and Vizianagaram. However, 30 to 40 per cent of the respondents paid extra money for the services in the districts of Cuddapah and Kurnool; and just less than 20 per cent of the respondents in districts of Anantapur, East Godavari, Khammam, Krishna, Nellore and Vizianagaram expressed the same view.

The data indicates that 80 to 100 per cent of the respondents in the districts like Mahbubnagar, Medak, Nalgonda and Srikakulam visited Mee Seva just once to avail their services. Similar views were expressed by 40 to 60 per cent of the respondents in districts like Cuddapah, East Godavari, Guntur, Khammam, Nellore, Prakasam, and Vizianagaram; whereas 40 to 60 per cent of respondents in the districts like Chittoor, Cuddapah, Guntur, East Godavari, Guntur,

Karimnagar, Khammam, Nizamabad, Visakhapatnam, Vizianagaram, Warangal and West Godavari visited the Mee Seva centres twice to avail the services.

ISES Integrated

The top districts in good category are Nalgonda, Nizamabad and Visakhapatnam; followed by Guntur, Nellore and Warangal in okay category.

Table 4.10

Service-wise Analysis: ISES-Integrated

Service Name	*Name of the District*	*Good (%)*	*Name of the District*	*Okay (%)*	*Name of the District*	*Average (%)*
	Nalgonda	100	Guntur	100	Khammam	10
ISES-Integrated	Nizamabad	100	Nellore	100	Chittor	9
	Visakhapatnam	100	Warangal	80	Adilabad	8

Analysis: The data indicates that 80 to 100 per cent of the respondents expressed high levels of satisfaction in availing the services in districts like Anantapur, Chittoor, Cuddapah, Krishna, Kurnool, Mahbubnagar, Nalgonda, Nizamabad, Prakasam and Visakhapatnam. A similar view was expressed by 60 to 79 per cent of the respondents in the districts like East Godavari, Rangareddy, Srikakulam, Vizianagaram and West Godavari; whereas 50 to 70 per cent of the respondents have expressed feeling okay in districts like Adilabad, Hyderabad, Khammam, Krishna and Medak. Otherwise just less than 20 per cent of the respondents expressed dissatisfaction in the districts like Adilabad, Chittoor, Hyderabad and Khammam.

The data also indicate that all respondents in the districts of Anantapur, East Godavari, Karimnagar, Mahbubnagar, Medak, Nalgonda, Nizamabad, Prakasam, Rangareddy, Srikakulam, Visakapatnam, Warangal and West Godavari did not pay any extra money for availing Mee Seva services and the same was expressed by 80 to 99 per cent of the respondents in the districts of Adilabad, Chittoor, Guntur, Hyderabad, Khammam, Krishna, Kurnool, Nellore and Vizianagaram.

The data indicates that 60 to 80 per cent of the respondents in the districts like Anantapur, Cuddapah, Guntur, Karimnagar, Khammam, Medak and Nellore visited Mee Seva centre only once to avail the services. Meanwhile, 40 to 60 per cent of the respondents visited twice in the districts like Adilabad, East Godavari, Hyderabad, Prakasam, Vizianagaram and Warangal; whereas 20 to 40 per cent of the respondents visited thrice to avail their services in the districts of Chittoor, Cuddapah, Hyderabad, Krishna, Nizamabad and Visakhapatnam. However, less than 20 per cent of the respondents visited more than four times in few districts like Krishna, Hyderabad.

Family Member Certificate

The top districts in good category are Mahbubnagar, Nalgonda and Srikakulam followed by Hyderabad, Guntur and Karimnagar in okay category.

Table 4.11

Service-wise Analysis: Family Member Certificate

Service Name	*Name of the District*	*Good (%)*	*Name of the District*	*Okay (%)*	*Name of the District*	*Average (%)*
Family Member Certificate	Mahbubnagar	100	Hyderabad	87	Vizianaga-ram	19
	Nalgonda	100	Guntur	82	Nellore	13
	Srikakulam	100	Karimnagar	82	Khammam	9

Analysis: The data indicates that 80 to 100 per cent of the respondents in districts like Chittoor, East Godavari, Kurnool, Mahbubnagar, Nalgonda, Rangareddy, Srikakulam and Visakhapatnam expressed high levels of satisfaction towards Mee Seva services. Between 70 to 90 per cent of respondents in districts like Guntur, Hyderabad, Karimnagar, Medak, Nellore and Warangal expressed feeling okay towards these services. Just less than 20 per cent of the respondents in districts like Anantapur, Hyderabad Khammam, Krishna, Nellore and Vizianagaram expressed dissatisfaction for availing the Mee Seva services.

The data also indicate that 100 per cent of the respondents in Cuddapah, East Godavari, Guntur, Karimnagar, Krishna, Medak, Nellore, Nizamabad, Prakasam, Rangareddy, Srikakulam,

Visakhapatnam, Vizianagaram, Warangal and West Godavari did not pay any excess money to avail the services. And 80 to 90 per cent of the respondents in the districts like Adilabad, Anantapur, Chittoor, Hyderabad, Khammam, Mahbubnagar and Nalgonda have the similar view.

The data indicates that all respondents in Mahbubnagar visited Mee Seva only once to avail the services; 90 per cent of the respondents expressed similar views in the district of Srikakulam and around 75 per cent of the respondents in the districts of Adilabad and Vizianagaram also echoed the same views. In the districts of Medak and Nalgonda, more than 60 per cent of the respondents stated that they visited Mee Seva twice to avail their services. Between 40 to 60 per cent of the respondents echoed similar views in the districts of Chittor, East Godavari, Gnutur, Hyderabad, Krishna, Kurnool, Nizamabad and Prakasam.

FMB Copy

The top districts in the good category are Anantapur, Khammam and Nalgonda. The top districts in the okay category are Medak, Warangal and Krishna.

Table 4.12

Service-wise Analysis: FMB Copy

Service Name	*Name of the District*	*Good (%)*	*Name of the District*	*Okay (%)*	*Name of the District*	*Average (%)*
	Anantapur	100	Medak	90	Medak	10
FMB Copy	Khammam	100	Warangal	90	Prakasam	10
	Nalgonda	100	Krishna	75	Nellore	4

Analysis: The data indicates that 100 per cent of the respondents in districts like Anantapur, Nalgonda, Khammam, Nizamabad, Srikakulam and Visakhapatnam have expressed high levels of satisfaction in availing the Mee Seva services. Similar views were expressed by 60 to 80 per cent of the respondents in districts like Adilabad, East Godavari, Prakasam, Rangareddy and Vizianagaram; whereas 60 to 80 per cent of the respondents in districts like Cuddapah, Guntur, Karimnagar, Krishna and West Godavari have expressed feeling okay regarding the services. In districts like Adilabad, East Godavari, Prakasam, Rangareddy and Vizianagaram, 10 to 30 per cent expressed the same view.

The data also indicate that 100 per cent of the respondents in districts like Anantapur, East Godavari, Guntur, Karimnagar, Khammam, Kurnool, Mahbubnagar, Medak, Nalgonda, Nizamabad, Prakasam, Rangareddy, Srikakulam, Visakhapatnam, Vizianagaram, Warangal and West Godavari, expressed that they did not pay any excess money for availing Mee Seva services.

The data indicates that all the respondents in the districts of Adilabad, Anantapur, Mahbubnagar, Nalgonda, Srikakulam and Vizianagaram have visited Mee Seva centre only once to avail the services, whereas 80 per cent of the respondents in Warangal, around 75 per cent of the respondents in Kurnool, and around 60 per cent of the respondents in the districts of Chittor, Karimnagar and Krishna visited the centres twice to avail the services. Around 40 per cent of the respondents visited Mee Seva centres thrice in the districts of Rangareddy and Visakhapatnam.

Mutation

The top districts in good category are Chittor, Khammam and Mahbubnagar. These are followed by Warangal, Nellore and Guntur in okay category.

Table 4.13

Service-wise Analysis: Mutation

Service Name	*Name of the District*	*Good (%)*	*Name of the District*	*Okay (%)*	*Name of the District*	*Average (%)*
	Chittor	100	Warangal	100	Prakasam	20
Mutation	Khammam	100	Nellore	90	Guntur	10
	Mahbubnagar	100	Guntur	80	Nellore	10

Analysis: The data indicates that 100 per cent of the respondents in the districts like Chittoor, Khammam, Mahbubnagar, Nalgonda, Rangareddy, Srikakulam and Visakhapatnam showed high levels of satisfaction in availing their services at Mee Seva centre. A similar view was expressed by 60 to 80 per cent of the respondents in Cuddapah, East Godavari, Krishna, Nizamabad and West Godavari. However,

40 to 60 per cent of the respondents feel okay towards the Mee Seva services. Less than 20 per cent of the respondents in districts like Guntur, Medak, Nellore and Prakasam experienced dissatisfaction in availing the services.

The data also indicate that 100 per cent of the respondents in the districts like Chittoor, East Godavari, Khammam, Kurnool, Mahbubnagar, Nalgonda, Prakasam, Rangareddy, Srikakulam, Visakhapatnam, Warangal and West Godavari did not pay any excess money for availing the Mee Seva services. Between 70 to 90 per cent of the respondents in the districts like Adilabad, Anantapur, Guntur, Karimnagar, Medak, Krishna, Nellore, Nizamabad and Vizianagaram also expressed similar views.

The data indicates that 100 per cent respondents in Mahbubnagar, Srikakulam and West Godavari visited Mee Seva centre only once to avail the services. Similar views were expressed by 60 to 80 per cent of the respondents in districts like Anantapur, East Godavari, Khammam, Medak, Nalgonda and Nellore; whereas 40 to 60 per cent of the respondents in districts like Chittoor, Guntur, Karimnagar, Kurnool, Nizamabad, Rangareddy, Vizianagaram, and Warangal stated that they visited Mee Seva centre twice. Around 30 to 40 per cent of the respondents in the districts like Guntur, Kurnool and Rangareddy visited thrice to avail the services.

District-wise Analysis

District: Adilabad

Overall Satisfaction with Mee Seva Services

Under Category A Services [Figure 4.2(a)], around 59 per cent of the users who were contacted said that the services offered at the Mee Seva are good, while 37 per cent of them felt that the service delivery at Mee Seva Centres are okay, while only 4 per cent of them felt that the services at Mee Seva are average.

Under Category B services [Figure 4.2(b)], 52 per cent of the users who were contacted said that the services offered at Mee Seva are really good, while 47 per cent of them said that the service delivery at Mee Seva centres is okay. Only 1 per cent of the users said that the service delivery by Mee Seva is average.

Figure 4.2(a)

Overall Satisfaction-Category A

Figure 4.2(b)

Overall Satisfaction-Category B

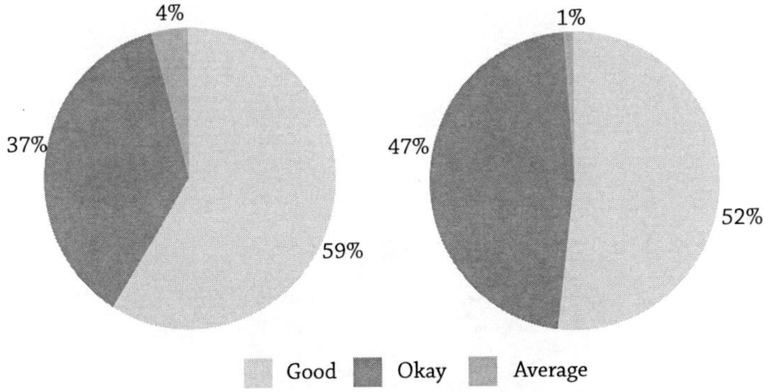

Number of Visits to Avail Services

Around 69 per cent of the citizens said that they visited the Mee Seva centres only once to get their work done, while 19 per cent said they visited twice, 6 per cent said they visited three times, and 4 per cent and 2 per cent of them said that they visited four times or more than four times respectively.

Figure 4.3

No. of Visits to Avail Services

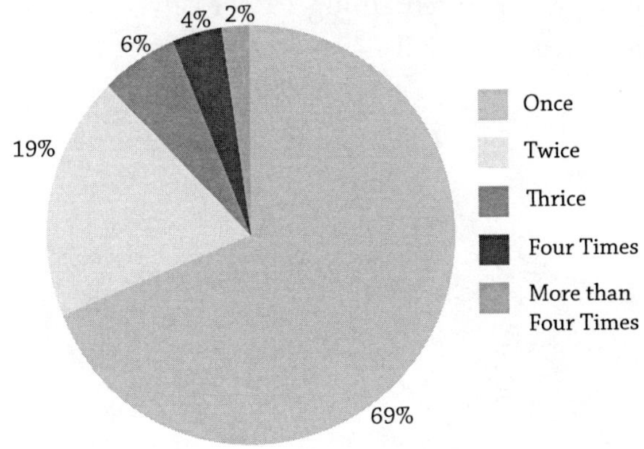

Paying Extra Money for Services

Around 88 per cent of the users who were contacted said that they did not have to pay any extra money to get their services from Mee Seva but around 12 per cent of the users said that they paid money for availing services from Mee Seva centres.

Figure 4.4

Paying Extra Money

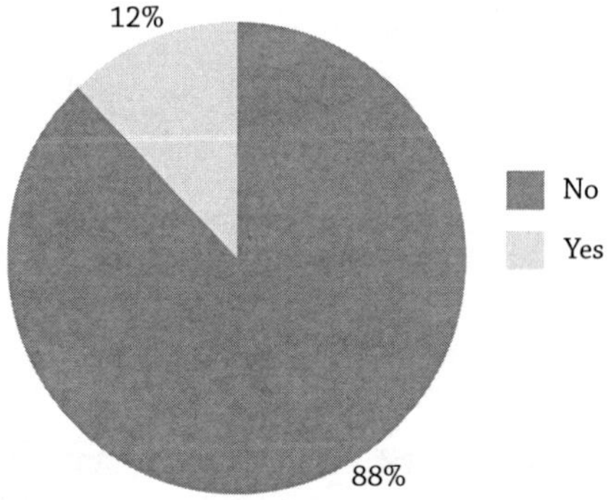

CSC Operators' View on the Reasons for Delay in Service Delivery

The study found that 38 per cent of them faced a delay in flow of information from the departments, 11 per cent stated that timelines were not adhered to, 19 per cent encountered attitudinal issues, 18 per cent of them found lack of interest in the government towards the programme, and the remaining 14 per cent of them stated lack of clarity in the procedures that have been instituted.

Figure 4.5

CSC Operators View

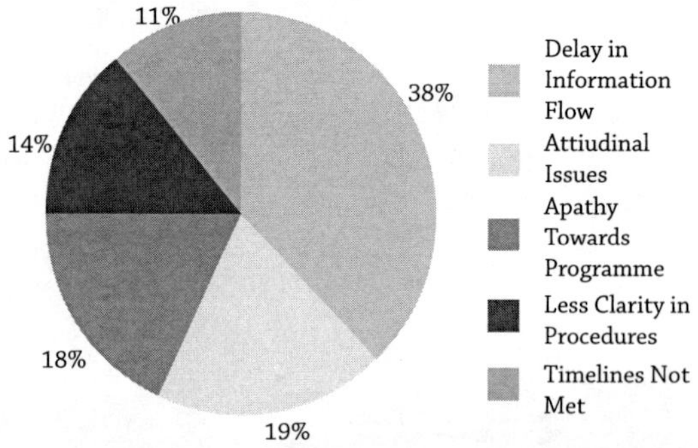

Observations by Field Teams

- People who visited the centres did not have much knowledge/information about the various services offered at the Mee Seva centres. This can be overcome by making the citizens aware of various services offered by Mee Seva through digital boards in those centres where there are a large number of transactions.
- Severe power cuts were witnessed and the backup was available for only two hours due to which citizens had to visit Mee Seva centres for more than three or four times to get their work done. The backup facility can be increased to at least four hours which can increase transaction speed. The operators at the centre are responsive and are helpful while transacting with the citizens. This is appreciable and commendable.

District: Anantapur

Overall Satisfaction with Mee Seva Services

Under Category A Services [Figure 4.6(a)], around 83 per cent of the users who were contacted said that the services offered at Mee Seva are good, while 17 per cent of them felt that the service delivery at Mee Seva centres is okay. None of them felt that the services at Mee Seva are average.

Under Category B Services [Figure 4.6(b)], around 67 per cent of the users who were contacted said that the services delivery at Mee Seva is good, while 31 per cent of them said that the service delivery at Mee Seva centres is okay. Only 2 per cent of the users said that the service delivery by Mee Seva is average.

Figure 4.6(a)

Overall Satisfaction-Category A

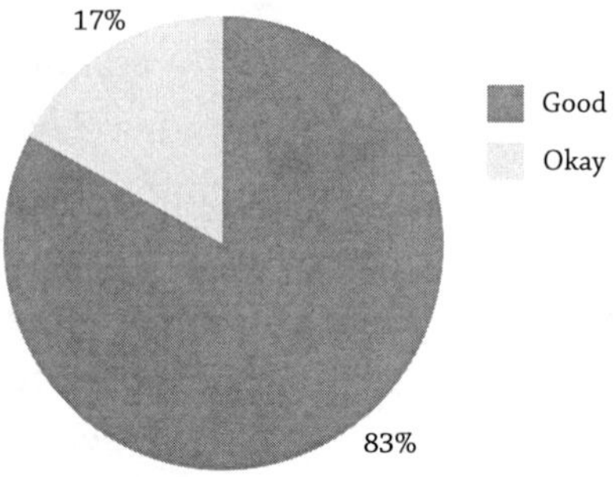

Figrue 4.6(b)

Overall Satisfaction-Category B

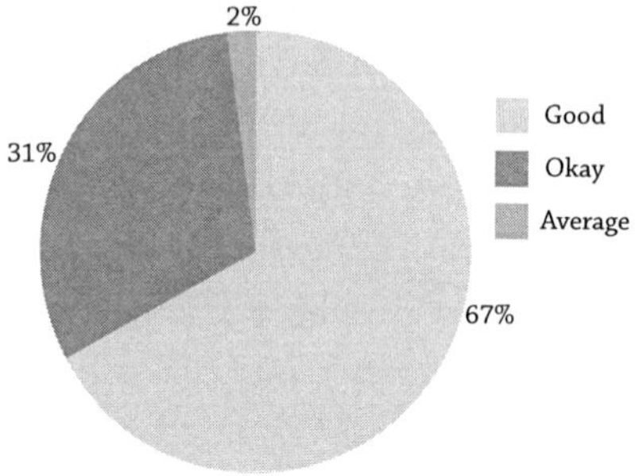

Number of Visits to Avail Services

Around 66 per cent of the citizens said that they visited the Mee Seva centres only once to get their work done; 21 per cent of them said that they visited twice; 6 per cent said that they visited three times; and 3 and 4 per cent of them said that they visited four times or more than four times for getting their work done at Mee Seva centres.

Figure 4.7

No. of Visits for Availing Services

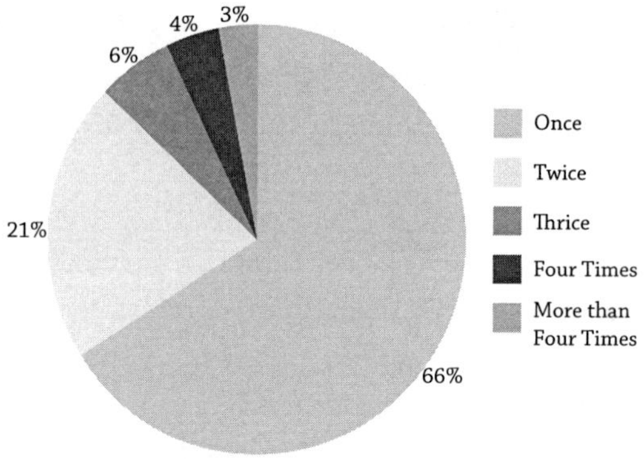

Paying Extra Money for Services

Around 89 per cent of the users who were contacted said that they did not have to pay any extra money to avail their services from Mee Seva, and around 11 per cent of the users said that they paid extra for availing services from Mee Seva centres.

Figure 4.8

Paying Extra Money

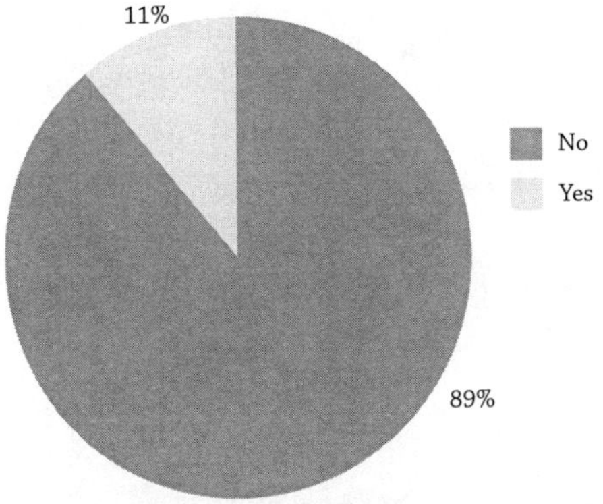

CSC Operators' View on the Reasons for Delay in Service Delivery

The CSC operators faced certain issues while delivering services to the citizens. The study found that 15 per cent of them faced a delay in flow of information from the departments, 23 per cent stated that timelines were not adhered to, 23 per cent encountered attitudinal issues, 31 per cent of them found lack of interest in the government towards the programme, and the remaining 8 per cent of them stated lack of clarity in the procedures that have been instituted.

Figure 4.9

CSC Operators' View

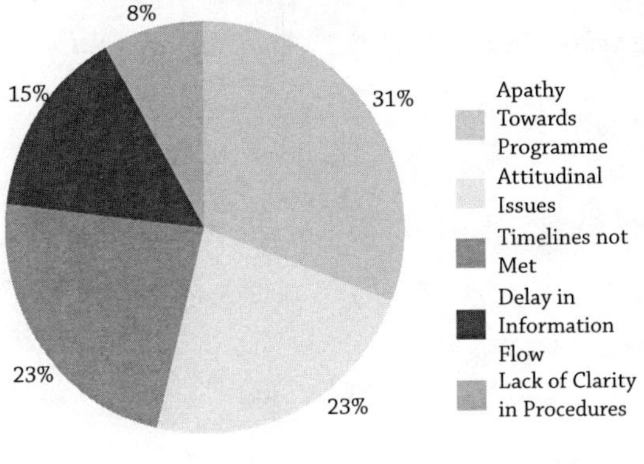

Observations by Field Teams

- The research team in the field observed that people have problems in getting Adangal/Pahani certificates. A number of citizens are using services like Income Certificate, Integrated Certificate, Residence Certificate, etc. In the Mee Seva centres visited, it was found that the inverters have backup power facility up to six hours. The same can be suggested for other centres with less backup facility. This will increase the number of transactions even during power shortages.

District: Chittor

Overall Satisfaction with Mee Seva Services

Under the Category A Services [Figure 4.10(a)], around 84 per cent of the users who were contacted said that the services offered at the Mee Seva are good, while 12 per cent of them felt that the service delivery at Mee Seva centres is okay, while only 4 per cent of them felt that the services at Mee Seva are average.

Under the Category B Services [Figure 4.10(b)], 78 per cent of the users who were contacted said that the services offered at Mee Seva are good, while 22 per cent of them said that the service delivery at Mee Seva centres is okay. None of the users said that the service delivery by Mee Seva is average.

Figure 4.10(a) *Overall Satisfaction-Category A*

Figure 4.10(b) *Overall Satisfaction-Category B*

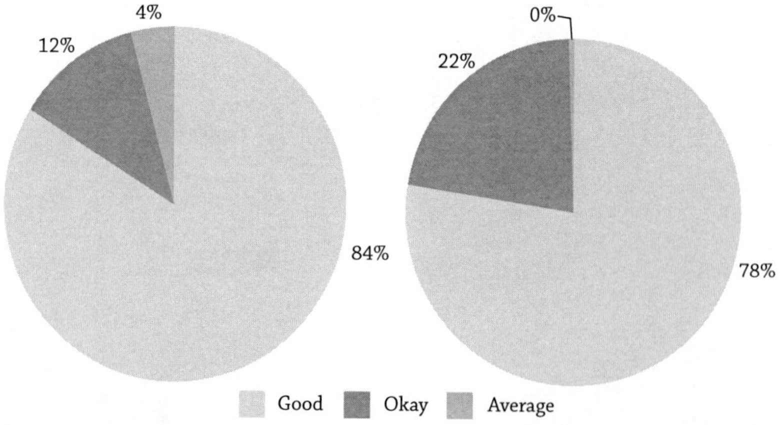

Number of Visits to Avail Services

Around 10 per cent of the citizens said that they visited the Mee Seva centres only once to get their work done, 50 per cent of them said that they visited twice, 27 per cent said that they visited three times, and 8 and 5 per cent of them said that they visited four times respectively or more than four times for getting their work done at Mee Seva centres.

Figure 4.11

No. of Visits to Avail Services

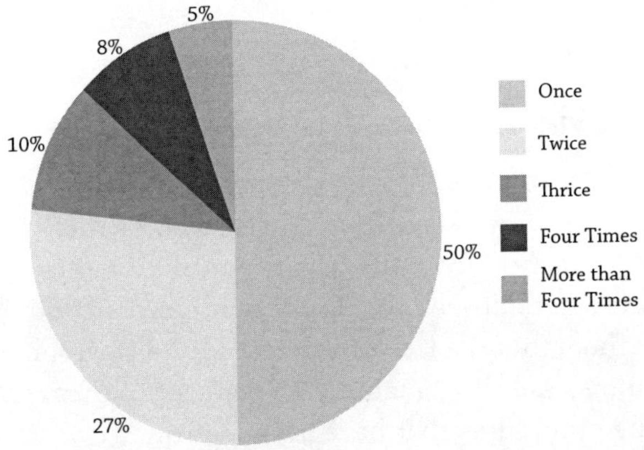

Paying Extra Money for Services

A question was raised on whether the citizens had to pay any extra money for accessing services from Mee Seva centres apart from the application fee. 96 per cent of the users who were contacted said that they did not pay any extra money to avail services from Mee Seva but around 4 per cent of the users said that they paid money for availing services from Mee Seva centres.

Figure 4.12

Paying Extra Money

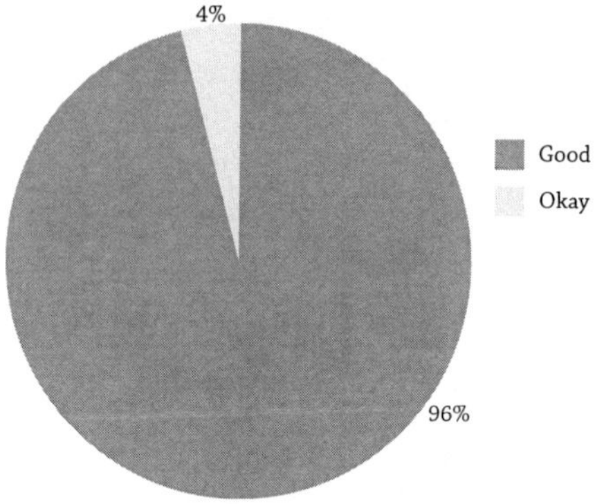

CSC Operators' View on the Reasons for Delay in Service Delivery

The CSC operators faced certain issues while delivering services to the citizens. The study found that 37 per cent of them faced a delay in flow of information from the departments, 15 per cent stated that timelines were not adhered to, 30 per cent faced attitudinal issues, 3 per cent of them found a lack of interest in the Government towards the programme, and the remaining 15 per cent of them stated lack of clarity in the procedures that have been instituted.

Figure 4.13

CSC Operators' View

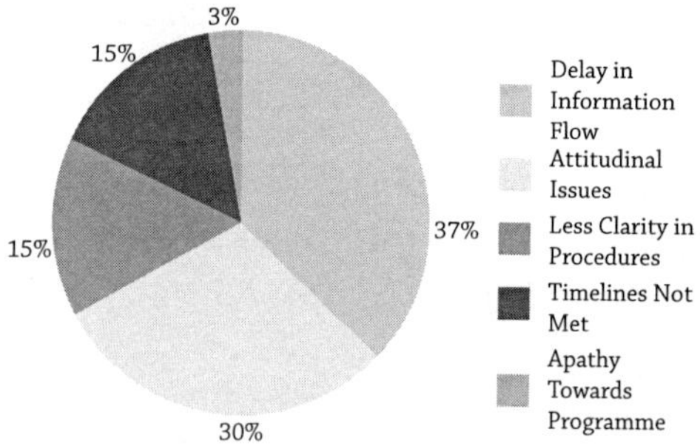

Observations by Field Teams

- Infrastructure problems, lack of stationery etc., were observed at few centres by the field staff. Display boards were not kept at the service centre leading to problems like the lack of information about the type and nature of services available at the centre.

- It was found that Mee Seva service messages were sent to customer mobiles in English. The illiterate people availing the services do not understand these messages. Thus, infrastructure facilities may be improved over a period of time and service messages may be sent in both English and Telugu.

District: Cuddapah

Overall Satisfaction with Mee Seva Services

Under Category A Services [Figure 4.14 (a)], around 69 per cent of the users who were contacted said that the services offered at the Mee Seva are good, while 31 per cent of them felt that the service delivery at Mee Seva centres is okay. None of them felt that the services at Mee Seva are average.

Under Category B Services [Figure 4.14(b)], around 70 per cent of the users who were contacted said that the services offered at Mee Seva are good, 28 per cent of them said that the service delivery at Mee Seva centres is okay and 2 per cent of them stated that the service delivery by Mee Seva is average.

Figure 4.14(a) *Overall Satisfaction-Category A*

Figure 4.14(b) *Overall Satisfaction-Category B*

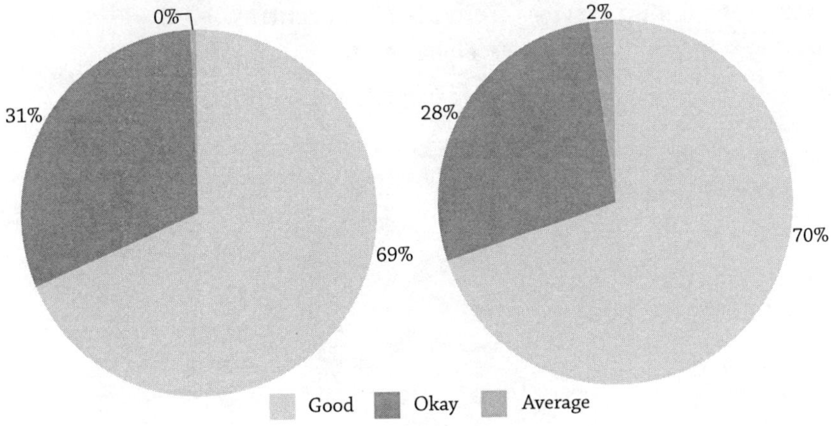

Number of Visits to Avail Services

Around 42 per cent of the citizens said that they visited Mee Seva centres only once to get their work done, 31 per cent of them said that they visited twice, 14 per cent said that they visited three times, while 4 per cent and 9 per cent of them said that they visited four times or more than four times respectively, for getting their work done at Mee Seva centres.

Figure 4.15

No. of Visits for Availing Services

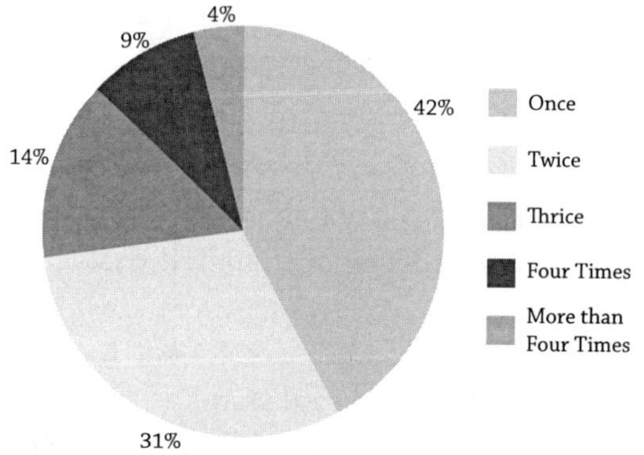

Paying Extra Money for Services

Around 88 per cent of the users who were contacted said that they did not have to pay any extra money to avail services from Mee Seva but around 12 per cent of the users said that they had paid money in terms for availing services from Mee Seva centres.

Figure 4.16

Paying Extra Money

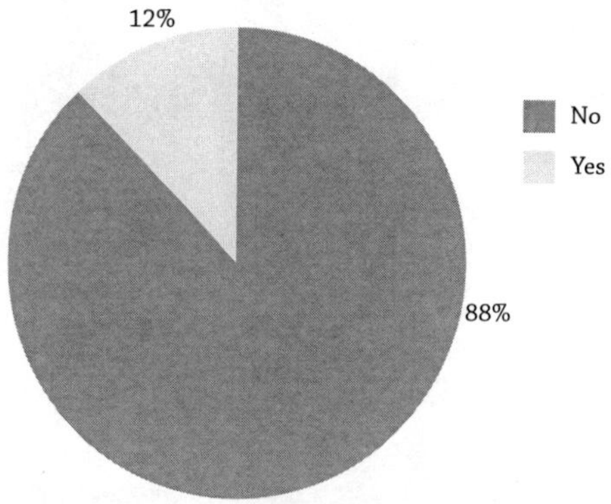

CSC Operators' View on the Reasons for Delay in Service Delivery

The study found that 40 per cent of them faced a delay in the flow of information from the departments, 10 per cent stated that timelines were not adhered to, 20 per cent encountered attitudinal issues, 20 per cent of them found a lack of interest in the government towards the programme, and the remaining 10 per cent of them stated lack of clarity in laid down procedures that have been instituted.

Figure 4.17

CSC Operators' View

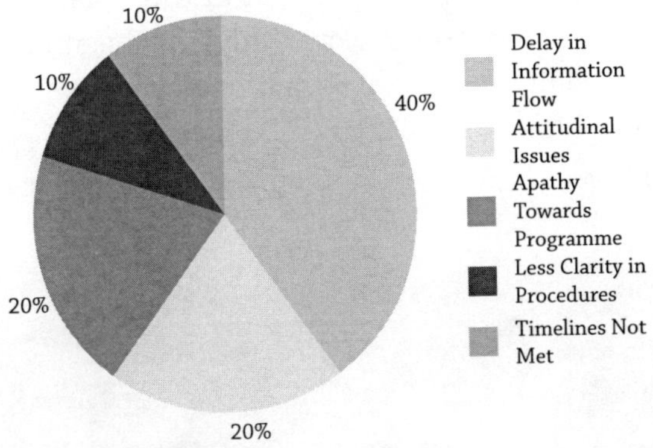

Observations by Field Teams

- The field observers found that the number of counters in the service centres were few (one to two) and there were server problems which caused delay in service delivery. It was also found that there were severe power cuts making it difficult for service centres to deliver services in the given time.
- The number of counters may be increased based on the number of transactions, and power shortages may be solved by using better inverters which can have a battery backup of at least three to four hours.

District: East Godavari

Overall Satisfaction with Mee Seva Services

Under the Category A Services [Figure 4.18(a)], around 64 per cent of the users who were contacted said that the services offered at the Mee Seva are good, while 31 per cent of them felt that the service delivery at Mee Seva centres is okay, while only 5 per cent of them felt that the services at Mee Seva are average.

Under the Category B Services [Figure 4.18(b)], around 64 per cent of the users who were contacted said that the services offered at Mee Seva are good, while 34 per cent of them said that the service delivery at Mee Seva centres is okay. Only 2 per cent of the users said that the service delivery by Mee Seva is average.

Figure 4.18(a) *Overall Satisfaction-Category A*

Figure 4.18(b) *Overall Satisfaction-Category B*

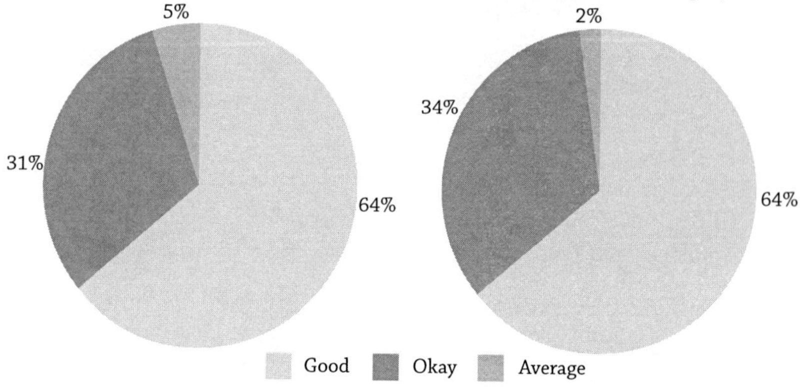

Number of Visits to Avail Services

Around 36 per cent of the citizens said that they visited Mee Seva centres only once to get their work done, 54 per cent of them said that they visited twice, 7 per cent said that they visited three times, while 2 per cent and 1 per cent of them said that they visited four times or more than four times respectively, for getting their work done at Mee Seva centres.

Figure 4.19

No. of Visits to Avail Services

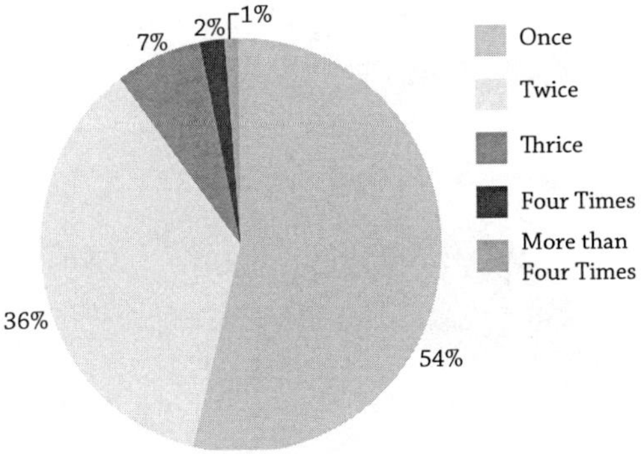

Paying Extra Money for Services

As a part of the survey, a question was raised on whether the citizens had to pay any extra money for availing services from Mee Seva centres apart from the application fee. Around 90 per cent of the users who were contacted said that they did not pay any extra money to get their services from Mee Seva but around 10 per cent of the users said that they paid extra for availing services from Mee Seva centres.

Figure 4.20

Paying Extra Money

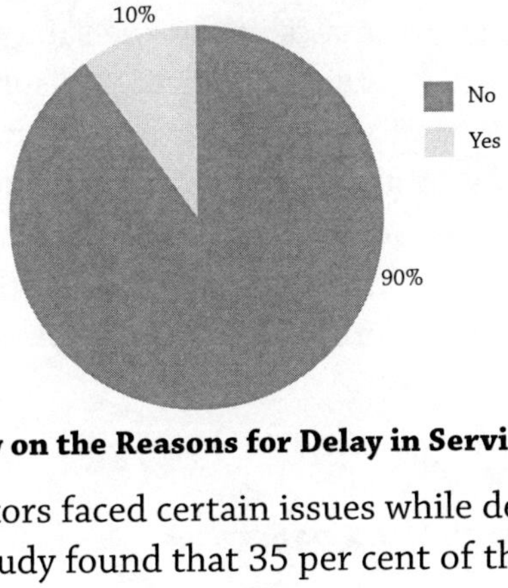

CSC Operators' View on the Reasons for Delay in Service Delivery

The CSC operators faced certain issues while delivering services to the citizens. The study found that 35 per cent of them faced a delay in the flow of information from the departments, 31 per cent stated that timelines were not adhered to, 14 per cent faced attitudinal issues, 9 per cent of them found a lack of interest in the Government towards the programme, and the remaining 11 per cent of them stated lack of clarity in the procedures that were instituted.

Figure 4.21

CSC Operators' View

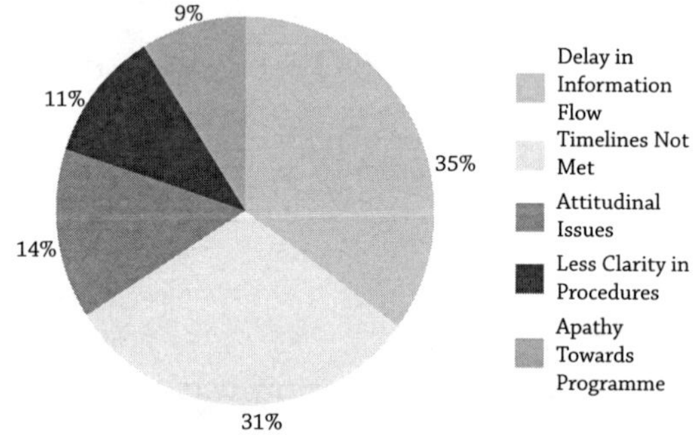

Observations by Field Teams

- The field observation was that connectivity problems are high and transactions are being delayed due to this problem. Certain Mee Seva centres are not following some of the guidelines regarding floor space, furniture etc.
- Some franchises are not providing chairs for customers. Further, it has been found that centre of Mee Seva neither has help desk facility, nor a cabin for the safety purpose to protect cash from theft. There was no proper display boards regarding the designations of the employees and thus making it difficult for the people to approach the right person for their issues. The centres may be given suitable guidelines with regard to the minimum facilities to be provided to the citizens and also the services being provided needs to be displayed for better visibility.

District: Guntur

Overall Satisfaction with Mee Seva Services

Under the Category A Services [Figure 4.22(a)], around 25 per cent of the users who were contacted said that the services offered at the

Mee Seva are good, 72 per cent of them felt that the service delivery at Mee Seva Centres is okay, while only 3 per cent of them felt that the services at Mee Seva are average.

Under the Category B Services [Figure 4.22(b)], around 35 per cent of the users who were contacted said that the services offered at Mee Seva are good, while 63 per cent of them said that the service delivery at the Mee Seva centres is okay and the rest 2 per cent said that the service delivery by Mee Seva is average.

Figure 4.22(a)

Overall Satisfaction-Category A

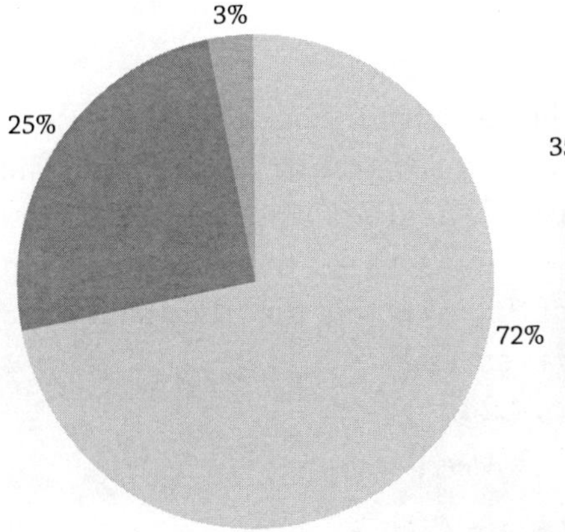

Figure 4.22(b)

Overall Satisfaction-Category B

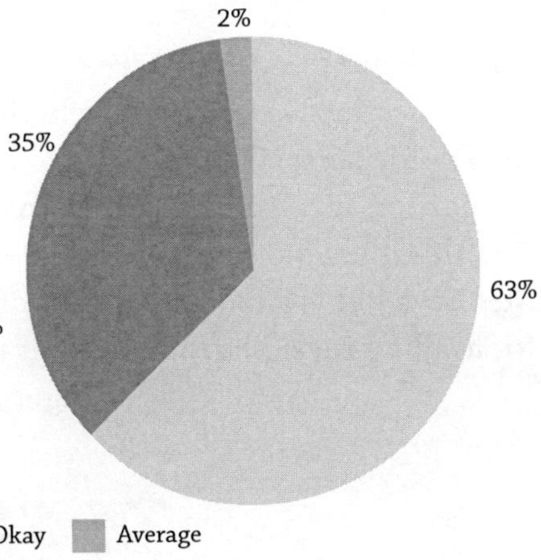

Number of Visits to Avail Services

Around 18 per cent of the citizens said that they visited the Mee Seva centres only once to get their work done, 44 per cent of them said that they visited twice, 22 per cent said that they visited three times, while 12 per cent and 4 per cent of them said that they visited four times or more than four times respectively, for getting their work done at Mee Seva centres.

Figure 4.23

No. of Visits to Avail Services

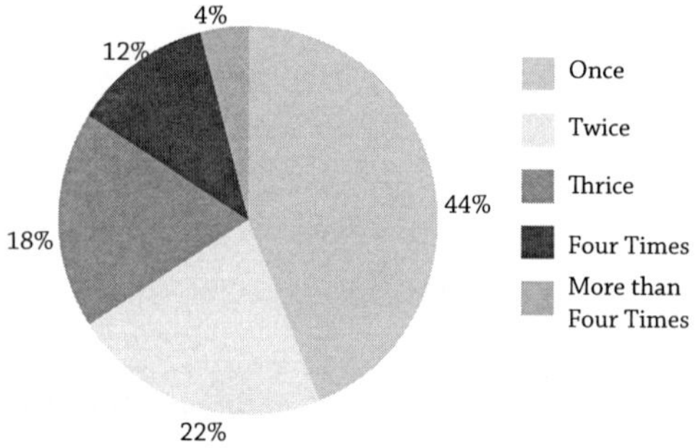

Paying Extra Money for Services

A question was raised on whether the citizens had to pay any extra money for accessing services from Mee Seva centres apart from the application fee. Around 89 per cent of the users who were contacted said that they did not pay any extra money to get their services from Mee Seva but around 11 per cent of the users said that they paid extra for availing services from Mee Seva centres.

Figure 4.24

Paying Extra Money

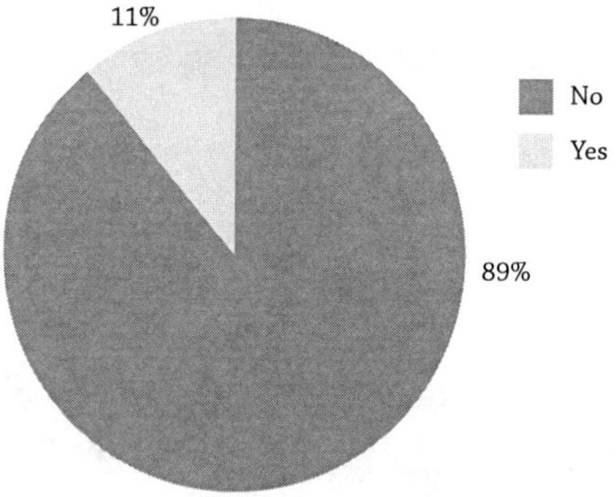

CSC Operators' View on the Reasons for Delay in Service Delivery

The CSC operators faced certain issues while delivering services to the citizens. The study found that 48 per cent of them faced a delay in the flow of information from the departments, 13 per cent stated that timelines were not adhered to, 12 per cent encountered

attitudinal issues, 9 per cent of them found a lack of interest in the Government towards the programme and the remaining 18 per cent of them stated lack of clarity in the procedures that have been instituted.

Figure 4.25

CSC Operators' View

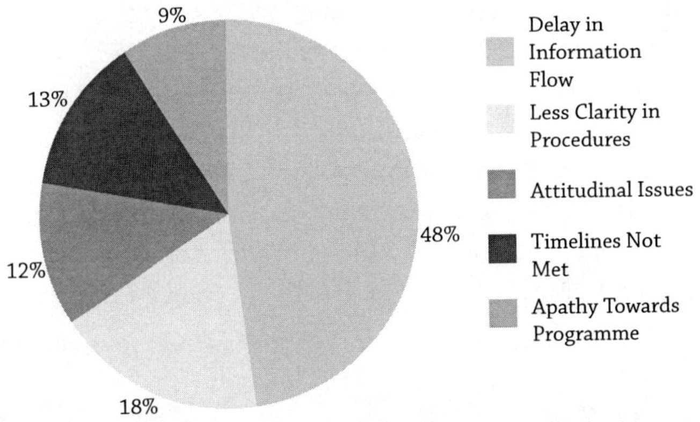

Observations by Field Teams

- The field observation is that operators of Mee Seva centres are cooperative with the citizens' and citizens are happy with the Mee Seva services being offered at the centres. However, no attempt made by any authority to generate awareness about the Mee Seva services among people.
- Certain Mee Seva centres do not have display boards. Therefore, people do not know or know clearly the services offered by the centre, and the timelines of the services. The centres may be suitably instructed to provide display boards. There is an urgent need to spread awareness among the people about the services being offered by the government. Print and electronic media can be used to generate awareness among citizens about the services being offered by Mee Seva.

District: Hyderabad

Overall Satisfaction with Mee Seva Services

Under the Category A Services [Figure 4.26(a)], around 50 per cent of the users who were contacted said that the services offered at the Mee Seva has been good, 45 per cent of them felt that the service delivery at Mee Seva Centres was okay, while only 5 per cent of them felt that the services at Mee Seva have been really bad.

Under the Category B Services [Figure 4.26(b)], around 47 per cent of the users who were contacted said that the services offered at Mee Seva are good, while 48 per cent of them said that the service delivery at Mee Seva centres is okay, and only 5 per cent of the users said that the service delivery by Mee Seva is average.

Figure 4.26(a)

Overall Satisfaction-Category A

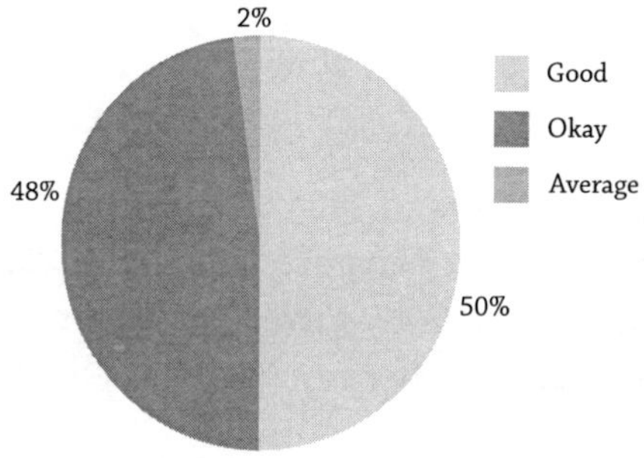

Figure 4.26(b)

Overall Satisfaction-Category B

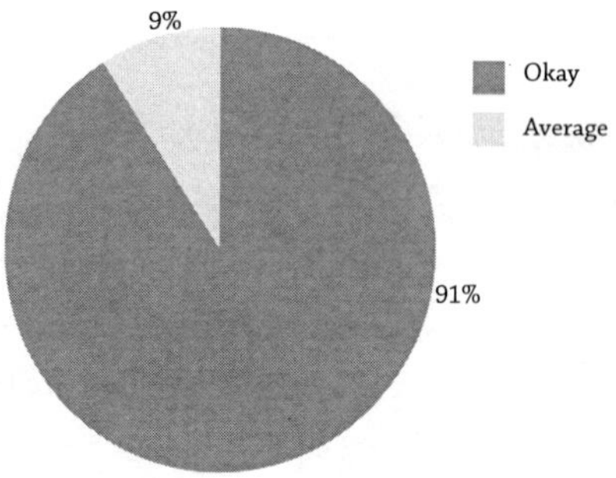

Number of Visits to Avail Services

Around 30 per cent of the citizens said that they visited the Mee Seva centres only once to get their work done, 33 per cent of them said that they visited twice, 16 per cent said that they visited three times, while 8 per cent and 13 per cent of them said that they visited four times or more than four times respectively, for getting their work done at Mee Seva centres.

Figure 4.27

No. of Visits to Avail Services

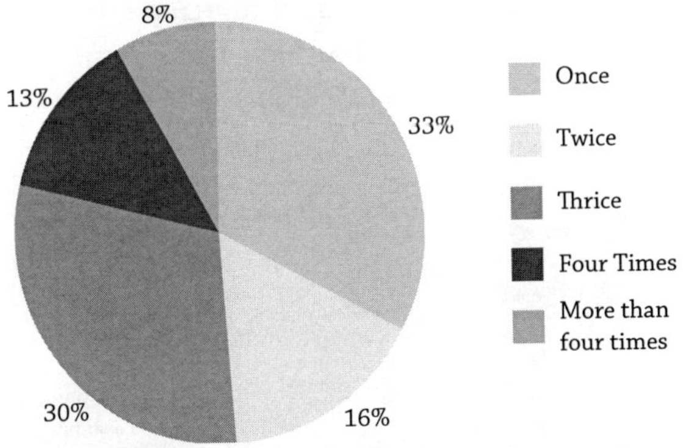

Paying Extra Money for Services

A question was raised on whether the citizens had to pay any extra money for accessing services from Mee Seva centres apart from the application fee. Around 92 per cent of the users who were contacted said that they did not pay any extra money to get their services from Mee Seva but around 8 per cent of the users said that they paid extra for accessing services from Mee Seva centres.

Figure 4.28

Paying Extra Money

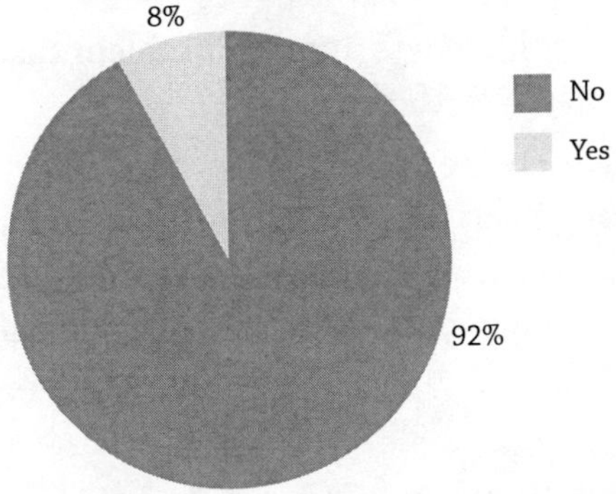

CSC Operators' View on the Reasons for Delay in Service Delivery

The CSC operators faced certain issues while delivering services to the citizens. The study found that 46 per cent of them faced a delay in the flow of information from the departments, 19 per cent stated that timelines were not adhered to, 12 per cent encountered attitudinal issues, 4 per cent of them found a lack of interest in the government towards the programme, and the remaining 19 per cent of them stated lack of clarity in the procedures that have been instituted.

Figure 4.29

CSC Operators' View

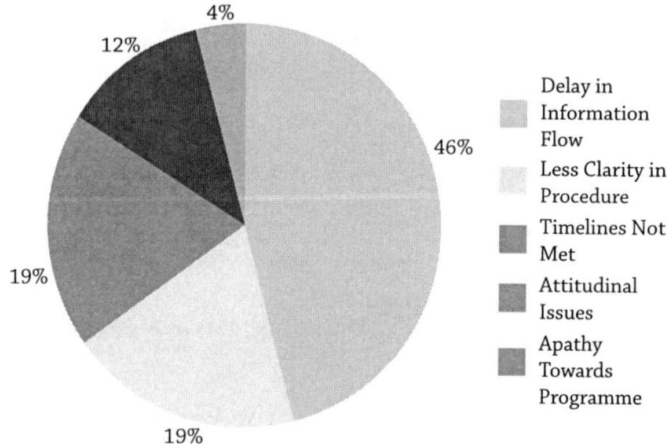

Observations by Field Teams

- The research team found that power shortage is a major problem because of which people are unable to avail their services. Although batteries are placed to overcome the problem, they are not sufficient to combat long hours of power cut. Server problem was another problem that led customers to be a bit unhappy with the delay.
- In CSCs, which are located in urban areas, there is a lot of crowd during peak hours. Customers were found to be waiting in long queues. The problems faced can be addressed if better inverters with longer back-up are placed at the centres.

District: Karimnagar

Overall Satisfaction with Mee Seva Services

Under the Category A Services [Figure 4.30(a)], around 42 per cent of the users who were contacted said that the services offered at the Mee Seva are good, while 58 per cent of them felt that the service delivery at Mee Seva centres is okay.

Under the Category B Services [Figure 4.30(b)], around 42 per cent of the users who were contacted said that the services offered at Mee Seva are good, while 57 per cent of them said that the service delivery at Mee Seva centres is okay. Only 1 per cent of the users said that the service delivery by Mee Seva is average.

Figure 4.30(a)

Overall Satisfaction-Category A

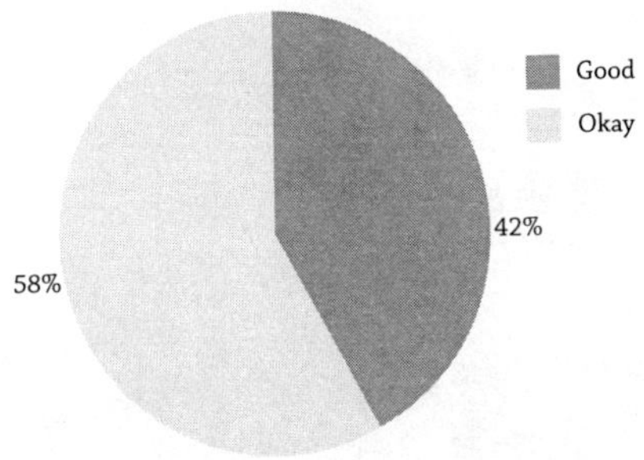

Figure 4.30(b)

Overall Satisfaction-Category B

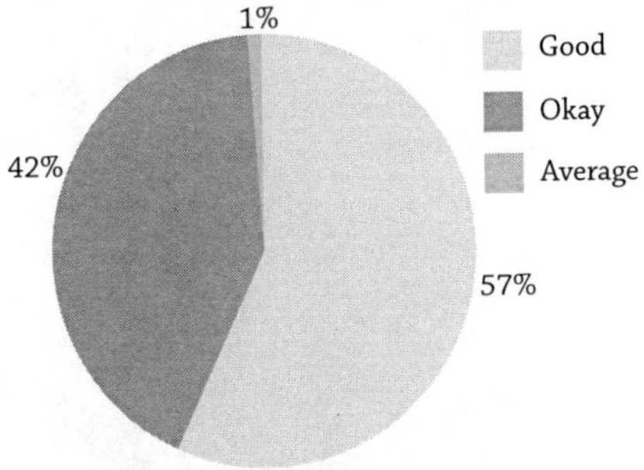

Number of Visits to Avail Services

Around 26 per cent of the citizens said that they visited the Mee Seva centres only once to get their work done, 38 per cent of them said that they visited twice, 21 per cent said that they visited three times, while 10 per cent and 5 per cent of them said that they visited four times or more than four times respectively, for getting their work done at Mee Seva centres.

Figure 4.31

No. of Visits to Avail Services

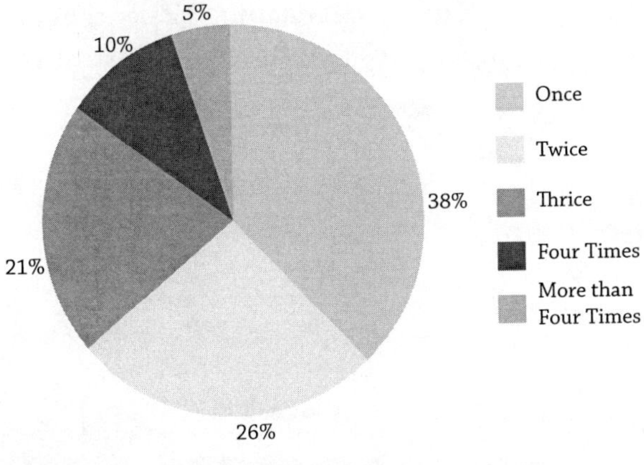

Paying Extra Money for Services

Around 94 per cent of the users who were contacted said that they did not pay any extra money to get their services from Mee Seva but around 6 per cent of the users said that they paid extra for availing services from Mee Seva centres.

Figure 4.32

Paying Extra Money

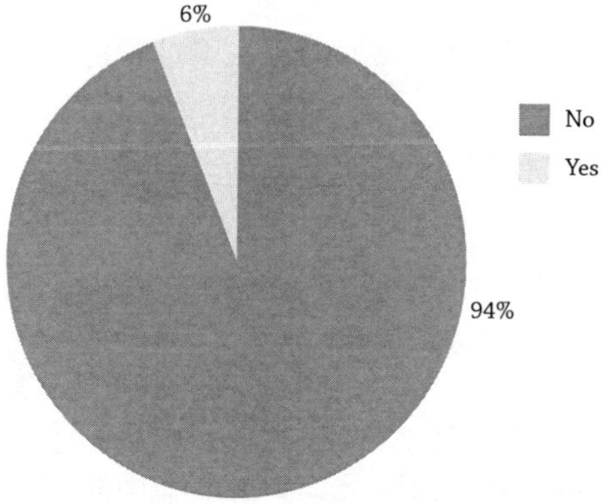

CSC Operators' View on the Reasons for Delay in Service Delivery

The CSC operators faced certain issues while delivering services to the citizens. The study found that 47 per cent of them faced a delay in the flow of information from the departments, 10 per cent stated that timelines were not adhered to, 22 per cent encountered attitudinal issues, 9 per cent of them found a lack of interest in the government towards the programme, and the remaining 12 per cent of them stated lack of clarity in the procedures that have been instituted.

Figure 4.33

CSC Operators' View

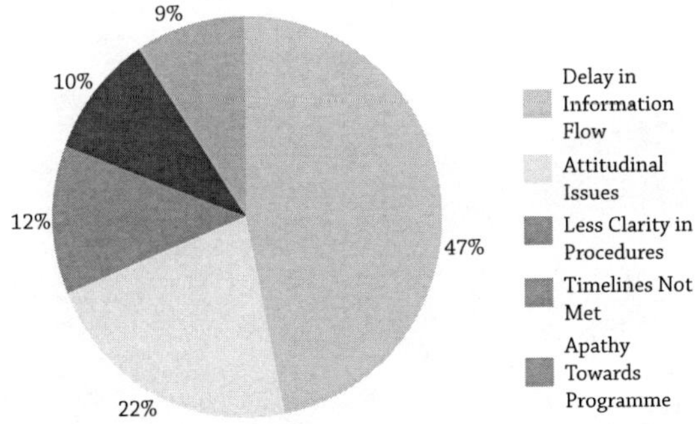

Observations by Field Teams

- Some of the Mee Seva centres, despite being located in main area, do not maintain proper infrastructure—number of chairs, ventilation, space, etc. The centres need to be given appropriate directions from time to time to maintain the infrastructure needed for providing services to the citizens.

District: Khammam

Overall Satisfaction with Mee Seva Services

Under Category A Services [Figure 4.34(a)], around 81 per cent of the users said that the services offered at Mee Seva are good, 16 per cent of them felt that the service delivery at Mee Seva centres is okay, while only 5 per cent of them felt that the services at Mee Seva are average.

Under Category B Services [Figure 4.34(b)], around 71 per cent of the users who were contacted said that the services offered at Mee Seva are good, while 25 per cent of them said that the service delivery at Mee Seva centres is okay. Only 4 per cent of the users said that the service delivery by Mee Seva is average.

Figure 4.34(a)

Overall Satisfaction-Category A

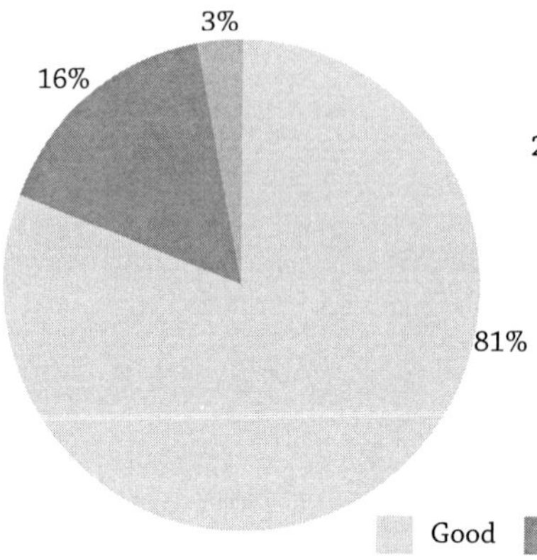

Figure 4.34(b)

Overall Satisfaction-Category B

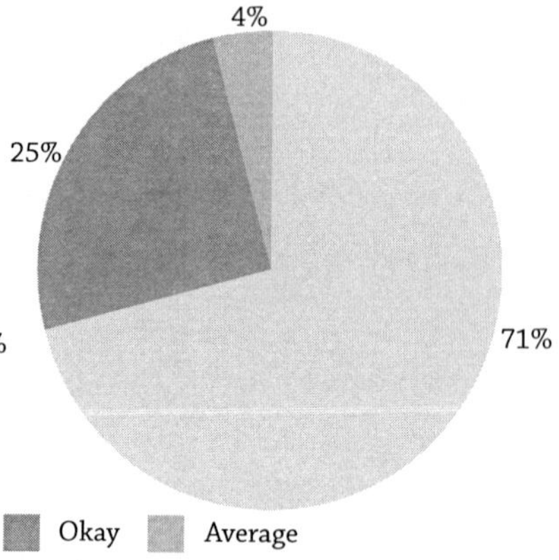

Number of Visits to Avail Services

Around 52 per cent of the citizens said that they visited the Mee Seva centres only once to get their work done, 35 per cent of them said that they visited twice, 6 per cent said that they visited three times, while 4 per cent and 3 per cent of them said that they visited four times or more than four times, respectively, for getting their work done at Mee Seva centres.

Figure 4.35

No. of Visits to Avail Services

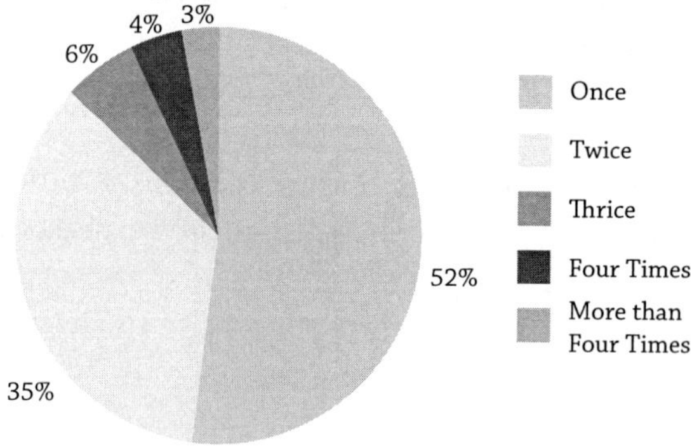

Paying Extra Money for Services

A question was asked whether the citizens had to pay any extra money for accessing services from Mee Seva centres apart from the application fee. Around 91 per cent of the users who were contacted said that they did not pay any extra money to get their services from Mee Seva but around 9 per cent of the users said that they paid extra for accessing services from Mee Seva centres.

Figure 4.36

Paying Extra Money

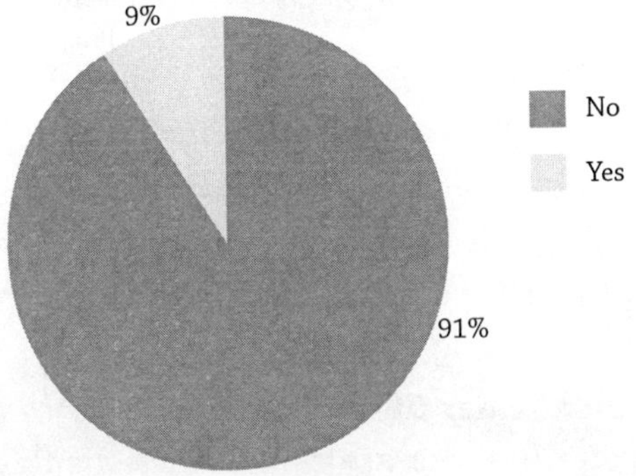

CSC Operators' View on the Reasons for Delay in Service Delivery

The CSC operators faced certain issues while delivering services to the citizens. The study found that 50 per cent of them faced a delay in the flow of information from the departments, 14 per cent stated that timelines were not adhered to, 18 per cent faced attitudinal issues, 6 per cent of them found a lack of interest in the government towards the programme, and the remaining 12 per cent of them stated lack of clarity in the procedures that have been instituted.

Figure 4.37

CSC Operators' View

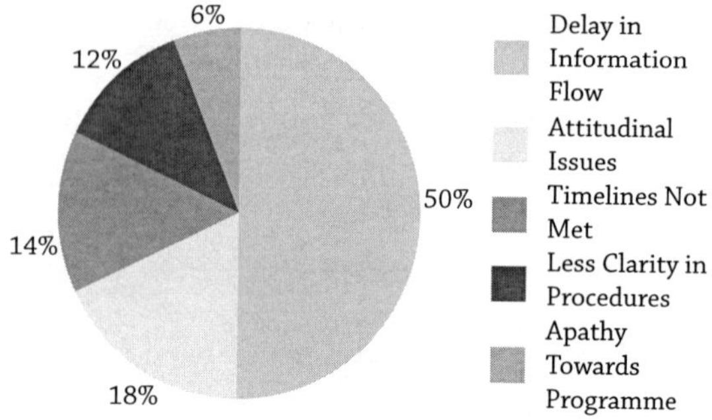

Observations by Field Teams

- The field observers found that there are frequent power cuts because of which people are unable to get their services. Although there are batteries, but due to long power cuts these do not run for a long duration.
- Some records under Current Adangal service are not updated and survey numbers are not clearly displayed forcing the citizens to come again and again to Mee Seva centre. Now that the data has been upgraded and digitised completely, the possibility of updated records not available does not arise. This apart, the focus is on providing clarity in the certificate providing survey numbers.

District: Krishna

Overall Satisfaction with Mee Seva Services

Under the Category A Services [Figure 4.38(a)], around 31 per cent of the users said that the services offered at the Mee Seva are good, 66 per cent of them felt that the service delivery at Mee Seva centres is okay, while only 3 per cent of them felt that the services at Mee Seva are average.

Under the Category B Services [Figure 4.38(b)], around 37 per cent of the users who were contacted said that the services offered at Mee Seva are good, while 58 per cent of them said that the service delivery at Mee Seva centres is okay. Only 5 per cent of the users said that the service delivery by Mee Seva is average.

Figure 4.38(a)

Overall Satisfaction-Category A

Figure 4.38(b)

Overall Satisfaction-Category B

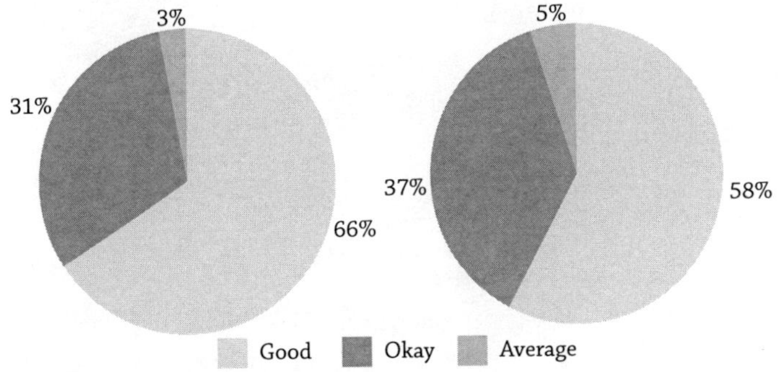

Number of Visits to Avail Services

Around 26 per cent of the citizens said that they visited the Mee Seva centres only once to get their work done, 46 per cent of them said that they visited twice, 17 per cent said that they visited three times, while 4 per cent and 7 per cent of them said that they visited four times or more than four times respectively, for getting their work done at Mee Seva centres.

Figure 4.39

No. of Visits to Avail Services

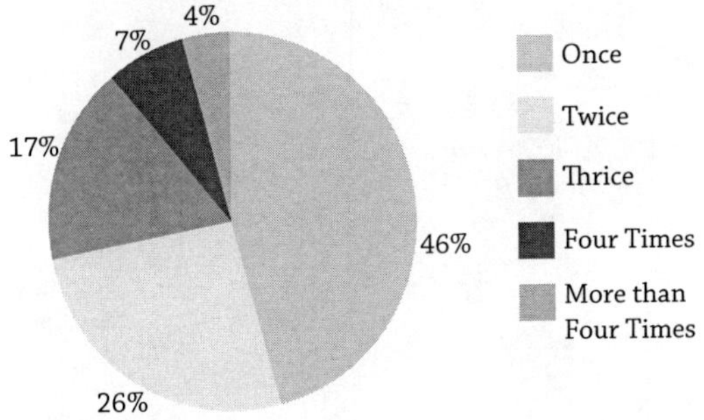

Paying Extra Money for Services

Around 90 per cent of the users who were contacted said that they did not pay any extra money to avail their services from Mee Seva but around 10 per cent of the users said that they paid extra for availing services from Mee Seva centres.

Figure 4.40

Paying Extra Money

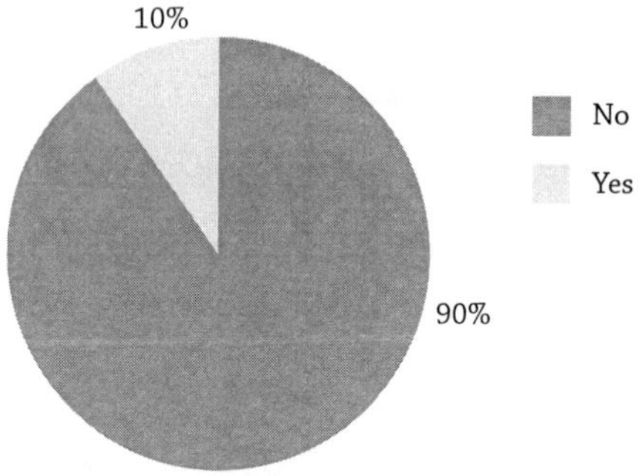

CSC Operators' View on the Reasons for Delay in Service Delivery

The CSC operators faced certain issues while delivering services to the citizens. The study found that 67 per cent of them faced attitudinal issues, 18 per cent of them encountered a delay in the flow of information from the departments, 5 per cent stated that timelines were not adhered to, 3 per cent of them found a lack of interest in the government towards the programme, and the remaining 7 per cent of them stated lack of clarity in the procedures that have been instituted.

Figure 4.41

CSC Operators View

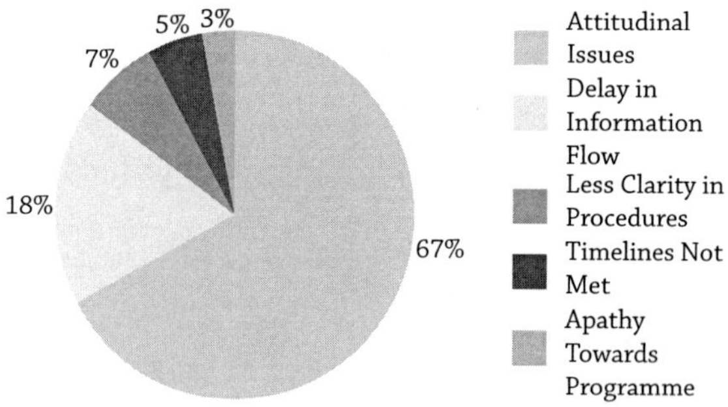

Observations by Field Teams

- The field observers found that power failure is a big problem in rural areas. Network connectivity issues and server issues are major problems too; and in some cases, there is not sufficient space and facilities available at the Mee Seva centres.

District: Kurnool

Overall Satisfaction with Mee Seva Services

Under Category A Services [Figure 4.42(a)], around 78 of the users who were contacted said that the services offered at the Mee Seva are good, while 22 per cent of them felt that the service delivery at Mee Seva Centres is okay.

Under Category B Services [Figure 4.42(b)], around 77 per cent of the users who were contacted said that the services offered at Mee Seva are good, while 21 per cent of them said that the service delivery at Mee Seva centres is okay. Only 2 per cent of the users said that the service delivery by Mee Seva is average.

Figure 4.42(a)

Overall Satisfaction-Category A

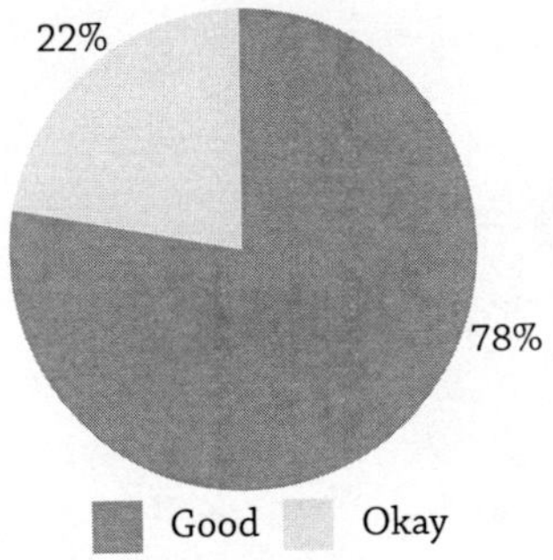

Figure 4.42(b)

Overall Satisfaction-Category B

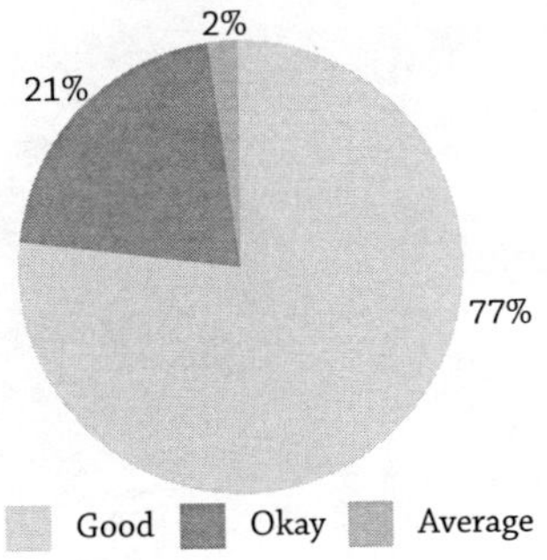

Number of Visits to Avail Services

Around 25 per cent of the citizens said that they visited the Mee Seva centres only once to get their work done, while 56 per cent of them said that they visited twice, 15 per cent said that they visited three times, while 3 per cent and 1 per cent of them said that they visited four times or more than four times respectively, for getting their work done at Mee Seva centres.

Figure 4.43

No. of Visits to Avail Services

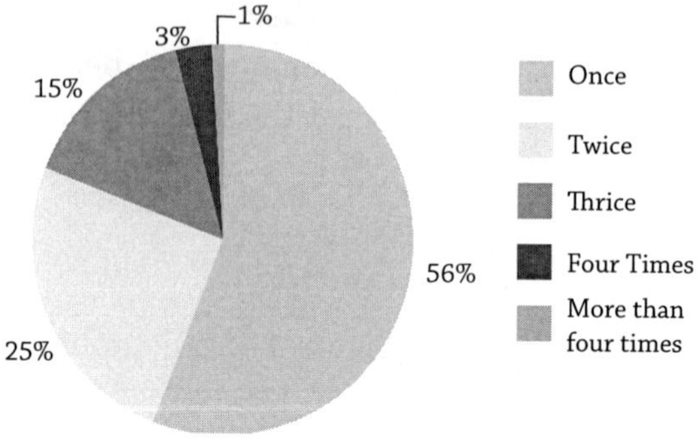

Paying Extra Money for Services

A question was raised on whether the citizens had to pay any extra money for accessing services from Mee Seva centres apart from the application fee. Around 94 per cent of the users who were contacted said that they did not pay any extra money to avail services from Mee Seva but around 6 per cent of the users said that they paid extra for availing services from Mee Seva centres.

Figure 4.44

Paying Extra Money

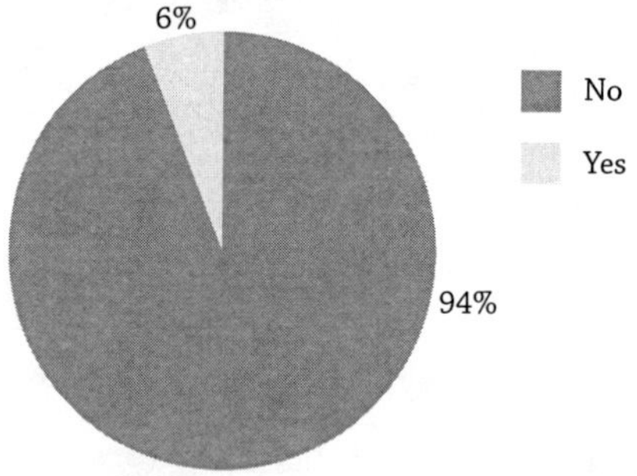

CSC Operators' View on the Reasons for Delay in Service Delivery

The CSC operators faced certain issues while delivering services to the citizens. The study found that 26 per cent of them faced a delay in the flow of information from the departments, 8 per cent stated that timelines were not adhered to, 32 per cent encountered

attitudinal issues, 17 per cent of them found a lack of interest in the Government towards the programme, and the remaining 17 per cent of them stated lack of clarity in the procedures that have been instituted.

Figure 4.45

CSC Operators' View

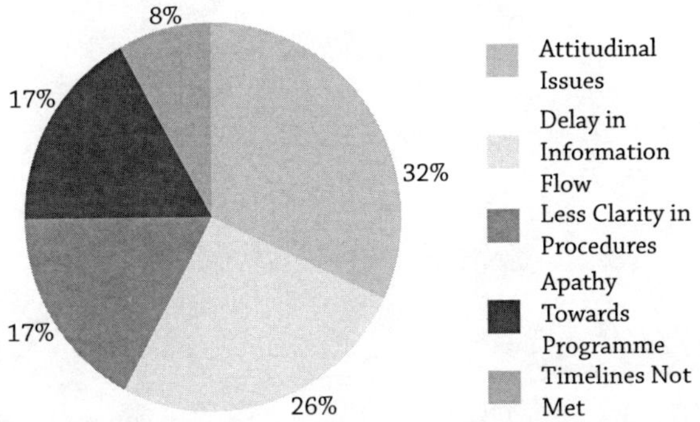

Observations by Field Teams

- The field observers found that some Mee Seva centres were facing network problem due to single server allocation to many branches, and infrastructure of Mee Seva centres was not satisfactory.
- Less space for seating and poor ventilation was found at some centres. However, the operators wre behaved courteously with the citizens.

District: Mahbubnagar

Overall Satisfaction with Mee Seva Services

Under the Category A Services [Figure 4.46(a)], around 84 per cent of the users who were contacted said that the services offered at the Mee Seva are good, while 16 per cent of them felt that the service delivery at Mee Seva Centres is okay.

Under the Category B Services [Figure 4.46(b)], around 91 per cent of the users who were contacted said that the services offered at Mee Seva are good, while 8 per cent of them said that the service delivery at Mee Seva centres is okay. Only 1 per cent of the users said that the service delivery by Mee Seva is average.

Figure 4.46(a)

Overall Satisfaction-Category A

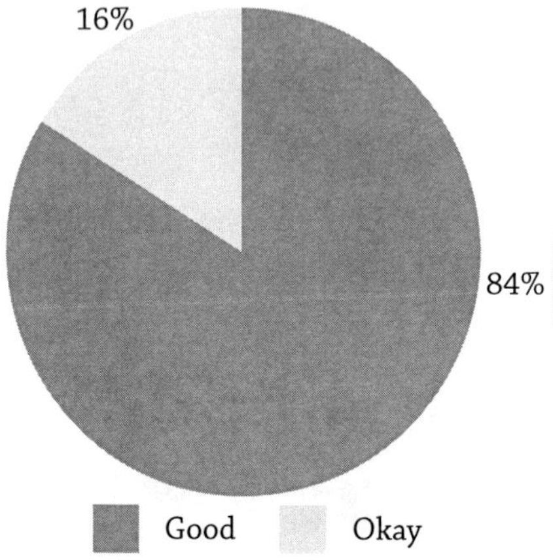

Figure 4.46(b)

Overall Satisfaction-Category B

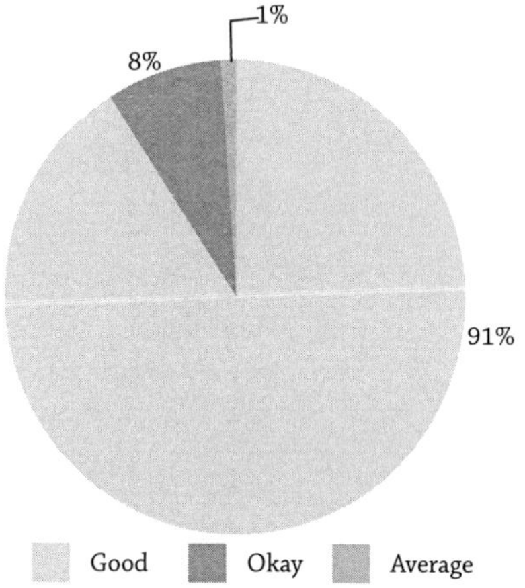

Number of Visits to Avail Services

Around 86 per cent of the citizens said that they visited the Mee Seva centres only once to get their work done, while 12 per cent of them said that they visited twice, and 2 per cent said that they visited three times for getting their work done at Mee Seva centres.

Figure 4.47

No. of Visits to Avail Services

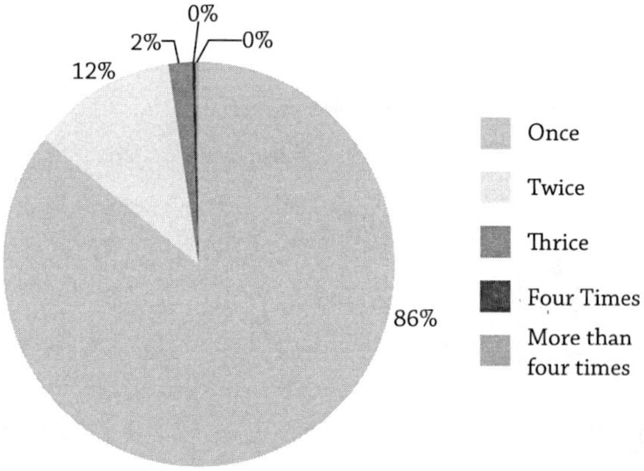

Paying Extra Money for Services

A question was raised on whether the citizens had to pay any extra money for accessing services from Mee Seva centres apart from the application fee. Around 99 per cent of the users who were contacted said that they did not pay any extra money to avail services from Mee Seva but around 1 per cent of the users said that they paid extra for availing services from Mee Seva centres.

Figure 4.48

Paying Extra Money

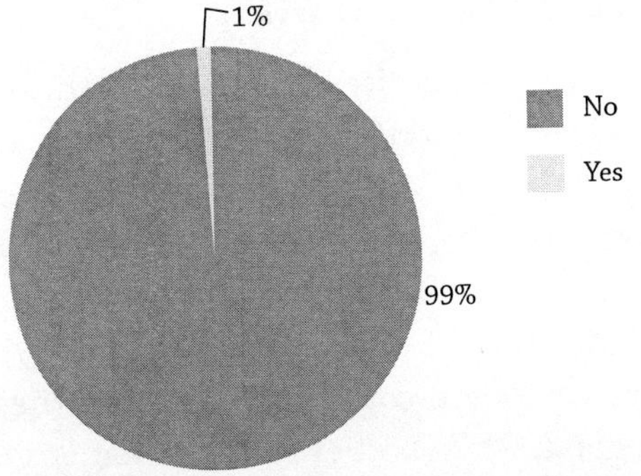

CSC Operators' View on the Reasons for Delay in Service Delivery

The CSC operators faced certain issues while the citizens. The study found that 60 per cent of them faced a delay in the flow of information from the departments, 10 per cent stated that timelines were not adhered to, and the remaining 30 per cent encountered attitudinal issues.

Figure 4.49

CSC Operators' View

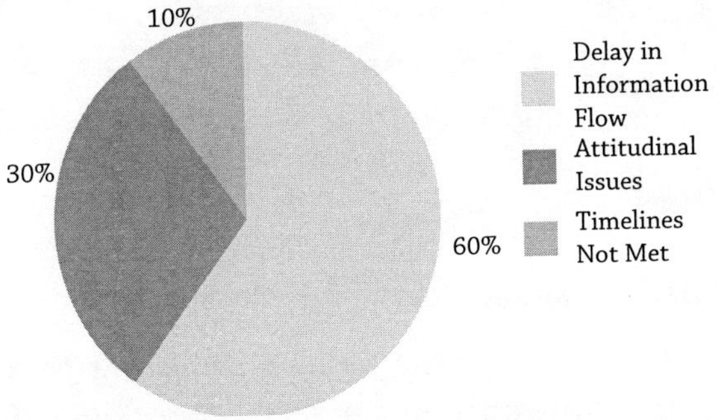

Observations by Field Teams

- Some of the services were not updated in the Mee Seva centres, even though listed in the services-offered list. The centres are unable to offer services like issuance of birth certificate and death certificate. Some Mee Seva centres are located in the same area within one kilometre distance leading to competition between the CSCs operators.

District: Medak

Overall Satisfaction with Mee Seva Services

Under the Category A Services [Figure 4.50(a)], around 23 per cent of the users who were contacted said that the services offered at the Mee Seva are good, 74 per cent of them felt that the service delivery at Mee Seva Centres is okay, while only 3 per cent of them felt that the services at Mee Seva are average.

Under the Category B Services [Figure 4.50(b)], around 42 per cent of the users who were contacted said that the services offered at Mee Seva are good, while 55 per cent of them said that the service delivery at Mee Seva centres is okay. Only 3 per cent of the users said that the service delivery by Mee Seva is average.

Figure 4.50(a)

Overall Satisfaction-Category A

Figure 4.50(b)

Overall Satisfaction-Category B

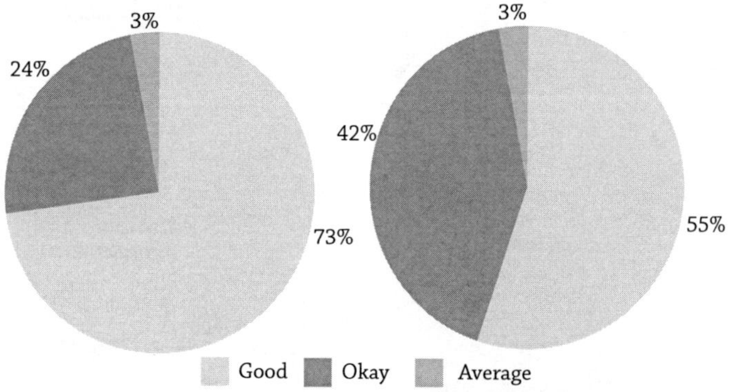

Number of Visits to Avail Services

Around 65 per cent of the citizens said that they visited the Mee Seva centres only once to get their work done, 26 per cent of them said that they visited twice, 6 per cent said that they visited three times, while 1 per cent and 2 per cent of them said that they visited four times or more than four times respectively, for getting their work done at Mee Seva centres.

Figure 4.51

No. of Visits to Avail Services

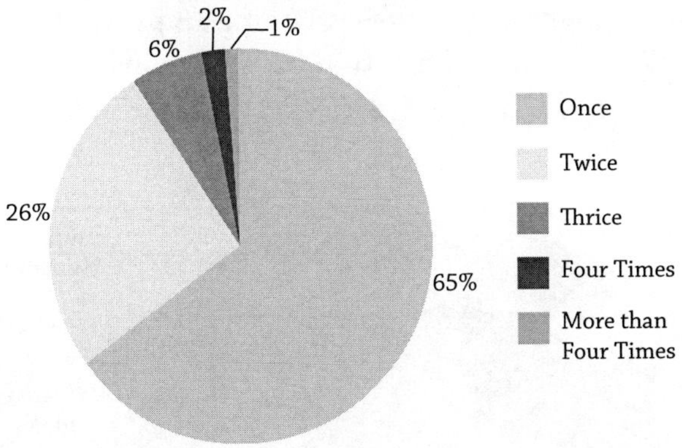

Paying Extra Money for Services

A question was raised on whether the citizens had to pay any extra money for accessing services from Mee Seva centres apart from the application fee. Around 98 per cent of the users who were contacted said that they did not pay any extra money to avail services from Mee Seva but around 2 per cent of the users said that they paid extra for availing services from Mee Seva centres.

Figure 4.52

Paying Extra Money

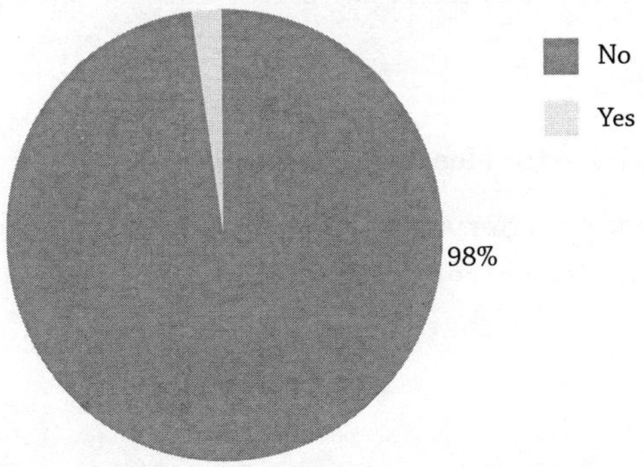

CSC Operators' View on the Reasons for Delay in Service Delivery

The CSC operators faced certain issues while delivering services to the citizens. The study found that 47 per cent of them faced a delay in the flow of information from the departments, 6 per cent stated that timelines were not adhered to, 23 per cent encountered attitudinal issues, 6 per cent of them found a lack of interest in the Government towards the programme, and the remaining 18 per cent of them stated lack of clarity in the procedures that have been instituted.

Figure 4.53

CSC Operators' View

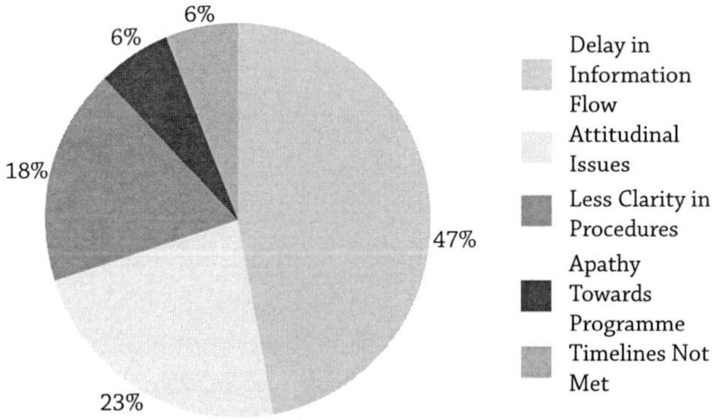

Observations by Field Teams

- The field observers found that Mee Seva centres were run by a good number of graduates, and that they are providing self-employment in rural places. Some customers stated that they received messages sent by the centres in English and were not able to understand. Some centres did not offer all the services.

District: Nalgonda

Overall Satisfaction with Mee Seva Services

Under Category A Services [Figure 4.54(a)], around 96 per cent of the users said that the services offered at the Mee Seva are good, while 4 per cent of them felt that the service delivery at Mee Seva Centres is okay.

Under Category B Services [Figure 4.54(b)], around 91 per cent of the users who were contacted said that the services offered at Mee Seva are good, while 8 per cent of them said that the service delivery at Mee Seva centres is okay. Only 1 per cent of the users said that the service delivery by Mee Seva is average.

Figure 4.54(a)

Overall Satisfaction-Category A

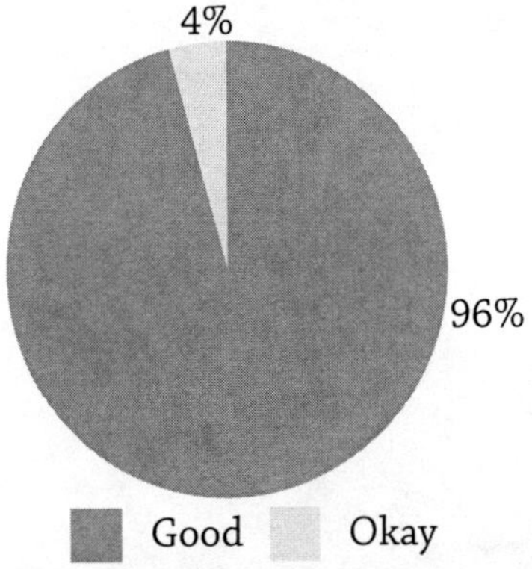

Figure 4.54(b)

Overall Satisfaction-Category B

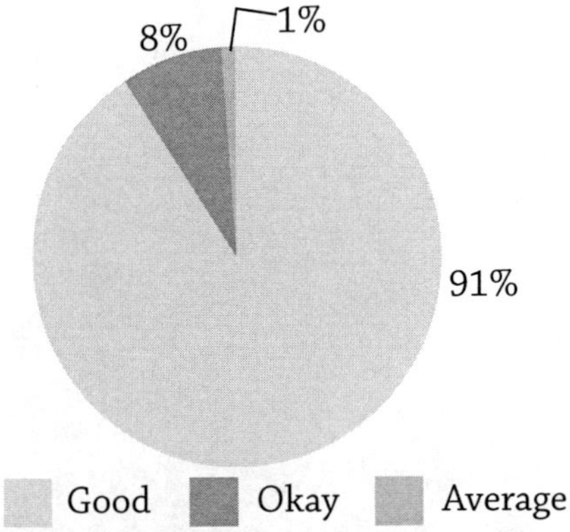

Number of Visits to Avail Services

80 per cent of the citizens said that they visited the Mee Seva centres only once to get their work done, 16 per cent of them said that they visited twice, 2 per cent said that they visited three times, while 1 per cent and 1 per cent of them said that they visited four times or more than four times respectively, for getting their work done at Mee Seva centres.

Figure 4.55

No. of Visits to Avail Services

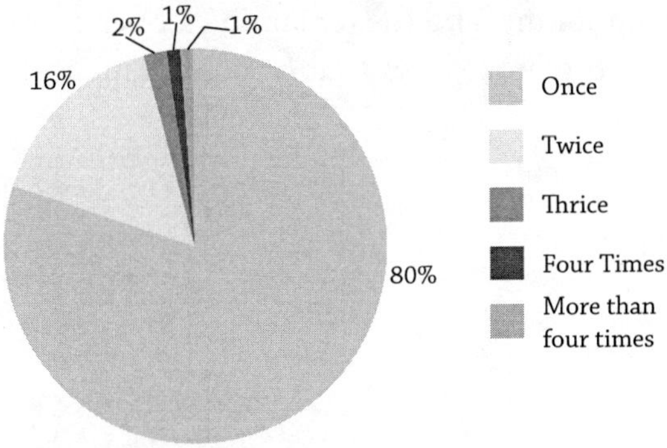

Paying Extra Money for Services

A question was raised whether the citizens had to pay any extra money for accessing services from Mee Seva centres apart from the application fee. 89 per cent of the users who were contacted said that they did not pay any extra money for availing services from Mee Seva but around 11 per cent of the users said that they had paid extra for availing services from Mee Seva centres.

Figure 4.56

Paying Extra Money

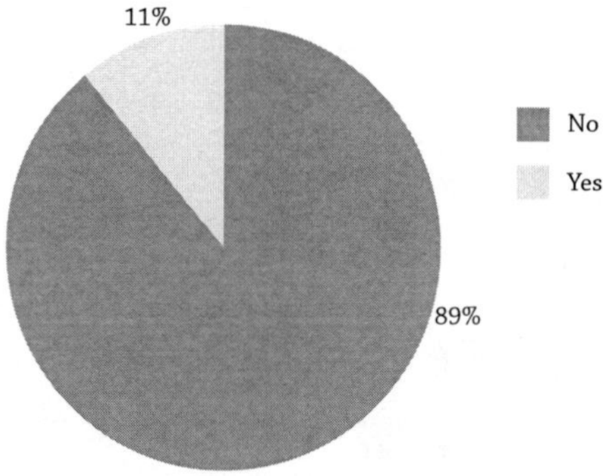

CSC Operators' View on the Reasons for Delay in Service Delivery

The CSC operators faced certain issues while delivering services to the citizens. The study found that 58 per cent of them faced a delay in the flow of information from the departments, 5 per cent stated that timelines were not adhered to, 10 per cent encountered attitudinal issues, 16 per cent of them found a lack of interest in the Government towards the programme, and the remaining 11 per cent of them stated lack of clarity in the procedures that have been instituted.

Figure 4.57

CSC Operators' View

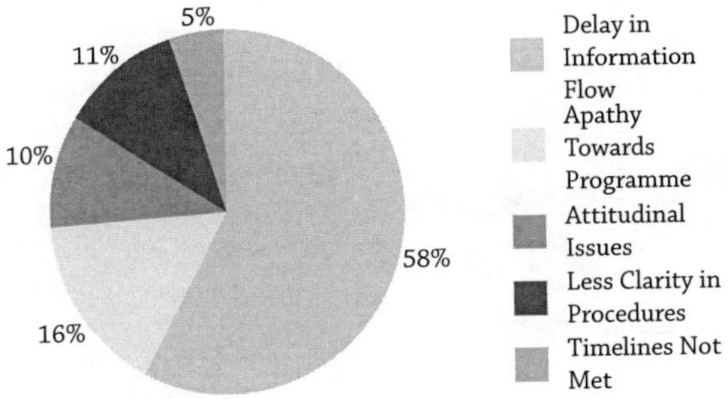

Observations by Field Teams

- The field observers found that Mee Seva centres in the district of Nalgonda are found to be following the guidelines provided by the Department of Information Technology, GoAP. Although, some CSCs were a bit crowded, the overall picture seems favourable towards the functioning of Mee Seva. That apart, the visuals of Mee Seva were displayed and the lighting facilities and other facilities were in place.

District: Nellore

Overall Satisfaction with Mee Seva Services

Under Category A Services [Figure 4.58(a)], around 23 per cent of the users who were contacted said that the services offered at the Mee Seva are good, 75 per cent of them felt that the service delivery at Mee Seva Centres is okay, while only 2 per cent of them felt that the services at Mee Seva are average.

Under the Category B Services [Figure 4.58(b)], around 24 per cent of the users who were contacted said that the services offered at Mee Seva are good, while 73 per cent of them said that the service delivery at Mee Seva centres is okay. Only 3 per cent of the users said that the service delivery by Mee Seva is average.

Figure 4.58(a)

Overall Satisfaction-Category A

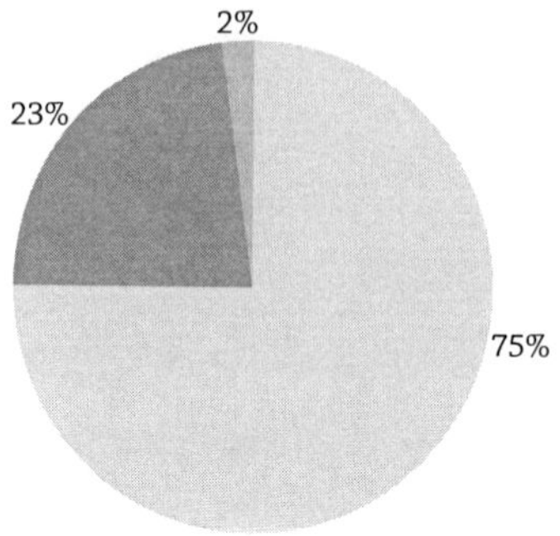

Figure 4.58(b)

Overall Satisfaction-Category B

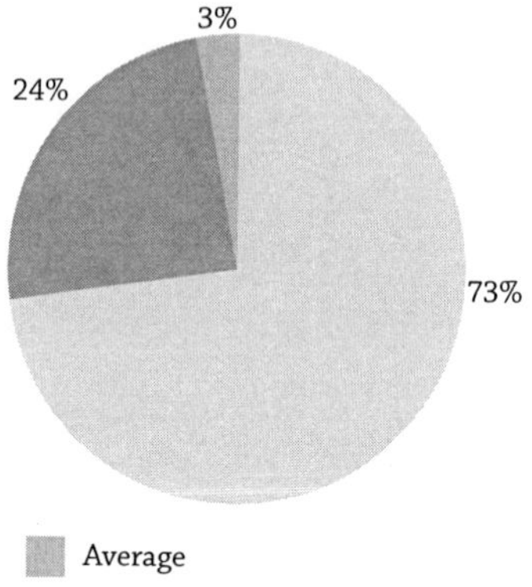

Number of Visits to Avail Services

Around 45 per cent of the citizens said that they visited the Mee Seva centres only once to get their work done, 21 per cent of them said that they visited twice, 9 per cent said that they visited three times, while 11 per cent and 14 per cent of them said that they visited four times or more than four times respectively, for getting their work done at Mee Seva centres.

Figure 4.59

No. of Visits to Avail Services

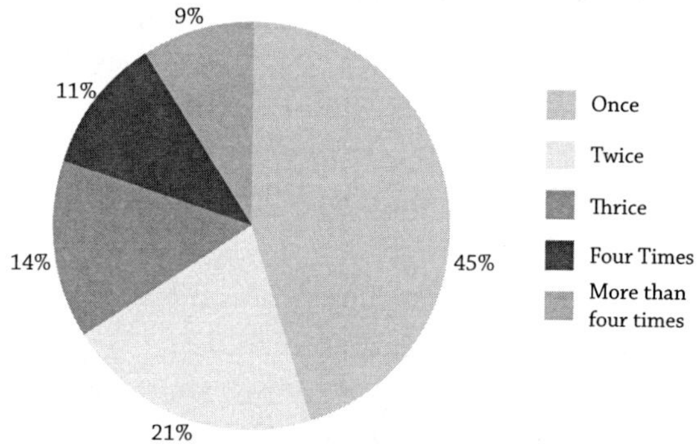

Paying Extra Money for Services

As a part of the survey, a question was raised on whether the citizens had to pay any extra money for accessing services from Mee Seva centres apart from the application fee. Around 93 per cent of the users who were contacted said that they did not pay any extra money to get their services from Mee Seva but around 7 per cent of the users said that they paid money for accessing services from Mee Seva centres.

Figure 4.60

Paying Extra Money

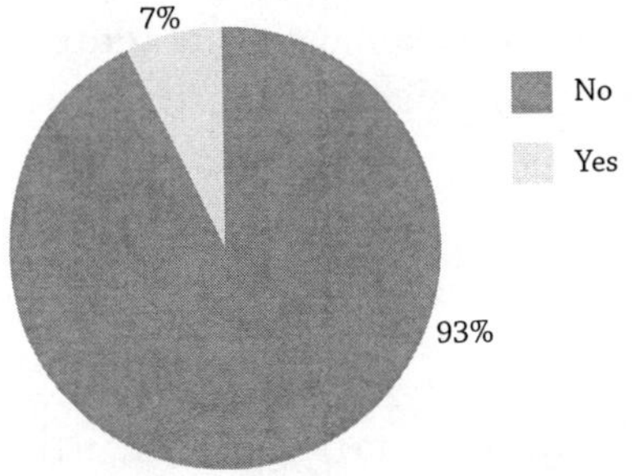

CSC Operators' View on the Reasons for Delay in Service Delivery

The CSC operators faced certain issues while delivering services to the citizens. The study found that 60 per cent of them faced a delay in the flow of information from the departments, 20 per cent encountered attitudinal issues, 7 per cent of them found a lack of interest in the Government towards the programme, and the remaining 13 per cent of them stated lack of clarity in the procedures that have been instituted.

Figure 4.61

CSC Operators' View

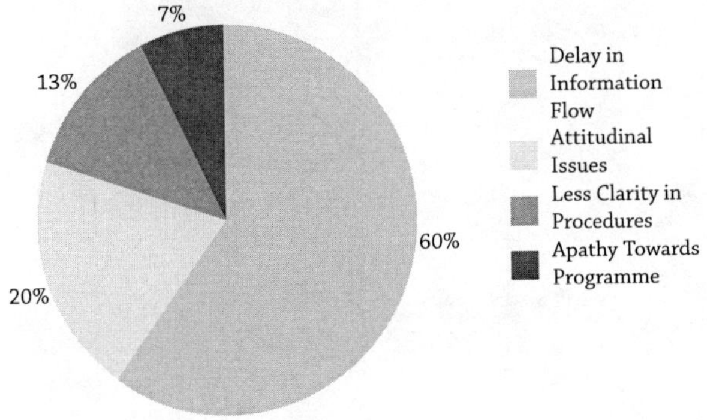

Observations by Field Teams

- The field observation was that in one of the centres applications were not available, and customers were asked to get applications from outside. There were complaints that they were not getting information at the right time for the delivery of services. Such issues have been addressed now by the EDS and the citizens no longer face such problems.

District: Nizamabad

Overall Satisfaction with Mee Seva Services

Under the Category A Services [Figure 4.62(a)], around 88 per cent of the users who were contacted said that the services offered at the Mee Seva are good, while 12 per cent of them felt that the service delivery at Mee Seva Centres is okay.

Under the Category B Services [Figure 4.62(b)], around 78 per cent of the users who were contacted said that the services offered at Mee Seva are good, while 18 per cent of them said that the service delivery at Mee Seva centres is okay. Only 4 per cent of the users said that the service delivery by Mee Seva is average.

Figure 4.62(a)

Overall Satisfaction-Category A

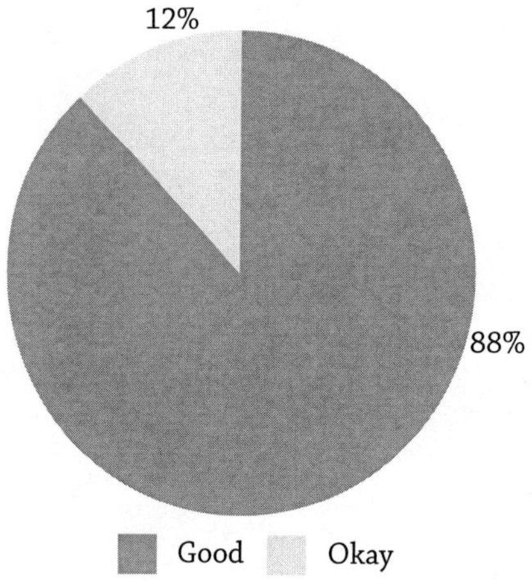

Figure 4.62(b)

Overall Satisfaction-Category B

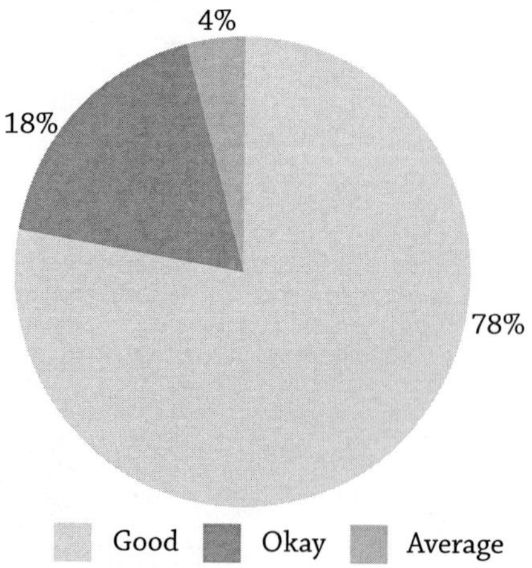

Number of Visits to Avail Services

Around 28 per cent of the citizens said that they visited the Mee Seva centres only once to get their work done, 37 per cent of them said that they visited twice, 21 per cent said that they visited three times, while 8 per cent and 6 per cent of them said that they visited four times or more than four times respectively, for getting their work done at Mee Seva centres.

Figure 4.63

No. of Visits to Avail Services

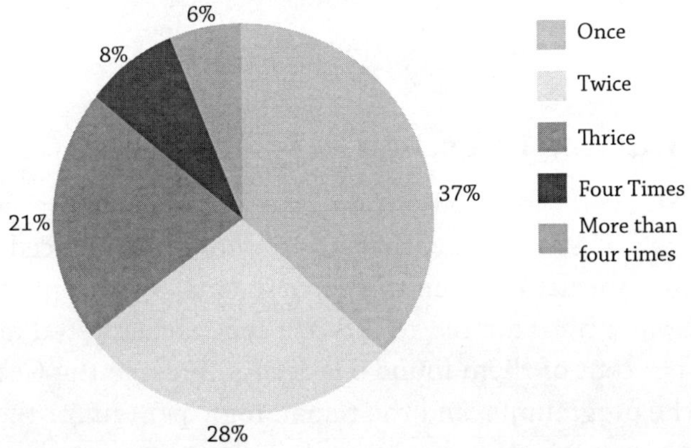

Paying Extra Money for Services

As a part of the survey, a question was raised on whether the citizens had to pay any extra money for accessing services from Mee Seva centres apart from the application fee. Around 96 per cent of the users who were contacted said that they did not pay any extra money to get their services from Mee Seva but around 4 per cent of the users said that they paid extra for accessing services from Mee Seva centres.

Figure 4.64

Paying Extra Money

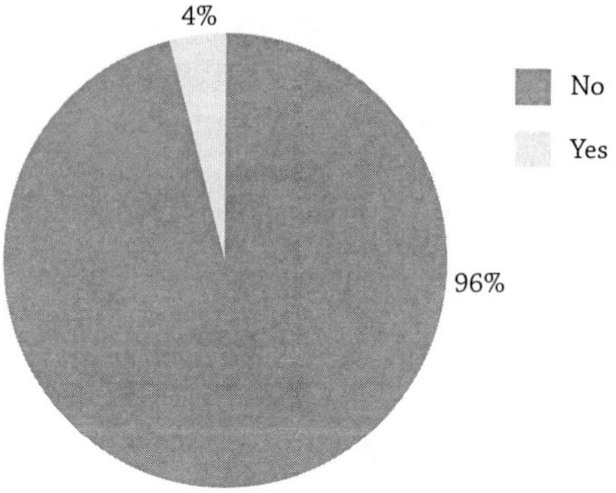

CSC Operators' View on the Reasons for Delay in Service Delivery

The CSC operators faced certain issues while delivering services to the citizens. The study found that 61 per cent of them faced a delay in the flow of information from the departments, 7 per cent stated that timelines were not adhered to, 18 per cent encountered attitudinal issues, 7 per cent of them found a lack of interest in the Government towards the programme, and the remaining 7 per cent of them stated lack of clarity in the procedures that have been instituted.

Figure 4.65

CSC Operators' View

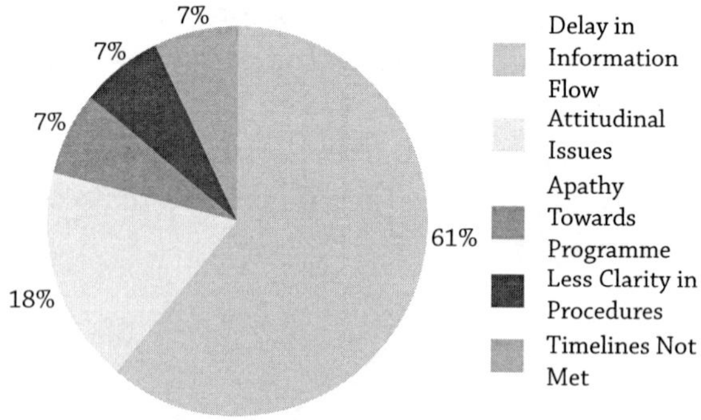

Observations by Field Teams

- The field observers found that some of urban Mee Seva centres have infrastructure as per the guidelines for the physical layout and specification of non-IT infrastructure. However, the server at most of the centres was slow, and the customers got irritated as they were forced to wait for a long time at the counter.

- The rural centres are smaller than the 150 sq feet and the logo is not placed as per the government regulations.

District: Prakasam

Overall Satisfaction with Mee Seva Services

Under Category A Services [Figure 4.66(a)], around 79 per cent of the users who were contacted said that the services offered at Mee Seva are good, 20 per cent of them felt that the service delivery at Mee Seva Centres is okay, while 3 per cent of them felt that the services at Mee Seva are average.

Under Category A Services [Figure 4.66(b)], around 69 per cent of the users said that the services offered at Mee Seva are good, while 29 per cent of them said that the service delivery at Mee Seva centres is okay. Only 2 per cent of the users said that the service delivery by Mee Seva is average.

Figure 4.66(a) *Overall Satisfaction-Category A*

Figure 4.66(b) *Overall Satisfaction-Category B*

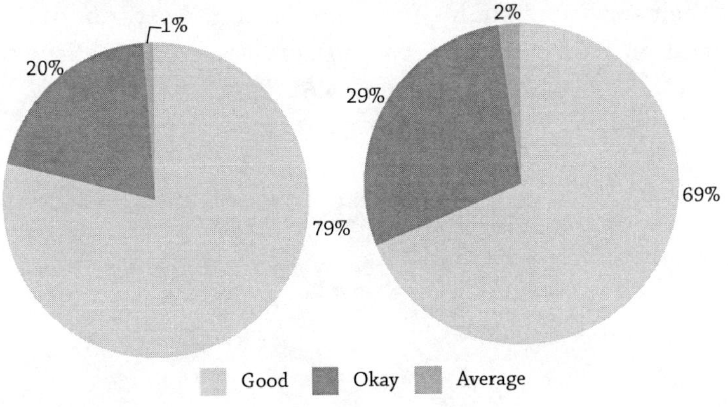

Number of Visits to Avail Services

Around 34 per cent of the citizens said that they visited the Mee Seva centres only once to get their work done, while 31 per cent of them said that they visited twice and 16 per cent said that they visited three times, while 6 per cent and 13 per cent of them said that they visited four times or more than four times respectively, for getting their work done at Mee Seva centres.

Figure 4.67

No. of Visits to Avail Services

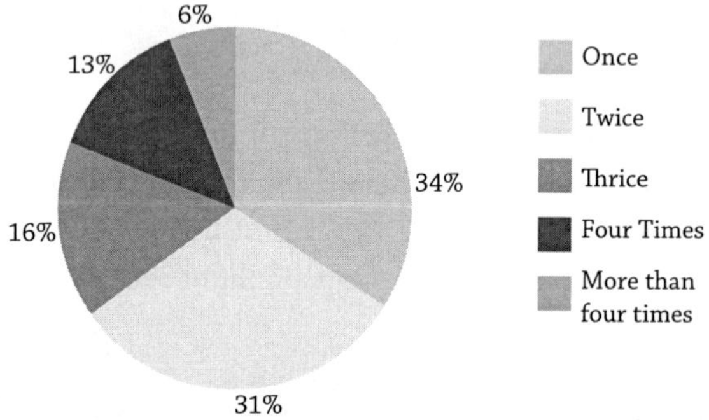

Paying Extra Money for Services

As a part of the survey, a question was raised on whether the citizens had to pay any extra money for accessing services from Mee Seva centres apart from the application fee. Around 97 per cent of the users who were contacted said that they did not pay any extra money to get their services from Mee Seva but around 3 per cent of the users said that they paid extra for accessing services from Mee Seva centres.

Figure 4.68

Paying Extra Money

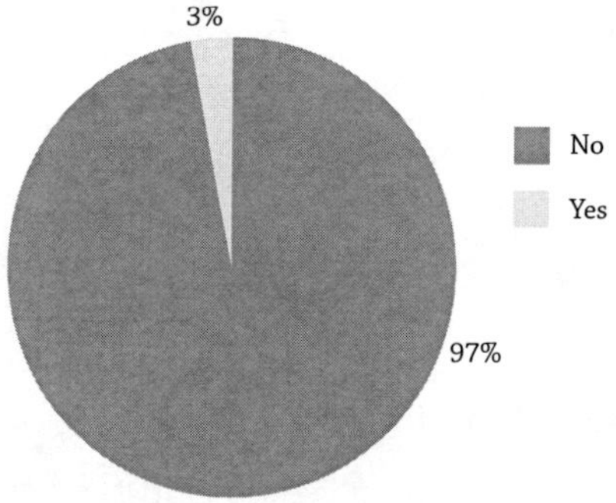

CSC Operators' View on the Reasons for Delay in Service Delivery

The CSC operators faced certain issues while delivering services to the citizens. The study found that 56 per cent of them faced a delay in the flow of information from the departments, 17 per cent stated that timelines were not adhered to, 13 per cent encountered attitudinal issues, 8 per cent of them found a lack of interest in the Government towards the programme, and the remaining 6 per cent of them stated lack of clarity in the procedures that have been instituted.

Figure 4.69

CSC Operators View

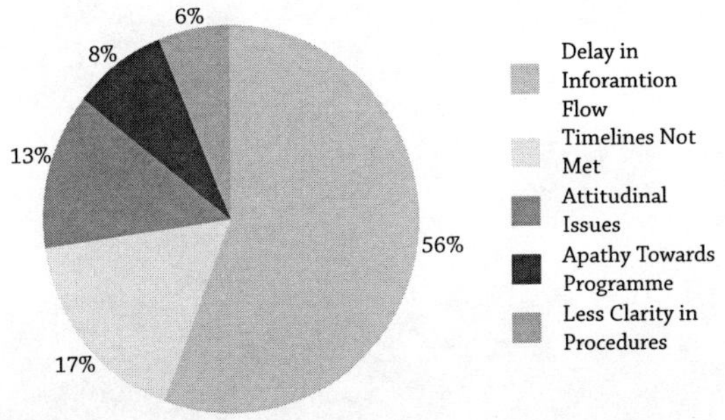

Observations by Field Teams

- The field team found that Mee Seva centres were well equipped and well furnished, and the centre had displayed the information boards about the Mee Seva services. The total strength of the employees was sufficient to serve the citizens better.
- The centre had good seating capacity. Operators had knowledge of the Mee Seva services and were handling separate services as assigned to them, thus resulting in the smooth functioning of the Mee Seva centre.

District: Rangareddy

Overall Satisfaction with Mee Seva Services

Under Category A Services [Figure 4.70(a)], around 73 per cent of the users who were contacted said that the services offered at the Mee Seva are good, 21 per cent of them felt that the service delivery at Mee

Seva Centres is okay, while 6 per cent of them felt that the services at Mee Seva are average.

Under Category B Services [Figure 4.70(b)], around 62 per cent of the users who were contacted said that the services offered at Mee Seva are good, while 37 per cent of them said that the service delivery at Mee Seva centres is okay. Only 1 per cent of the users said that the service delivery by Mee Seva is average.

Figure 4.70(a)

Overall Satisfaction-Category A

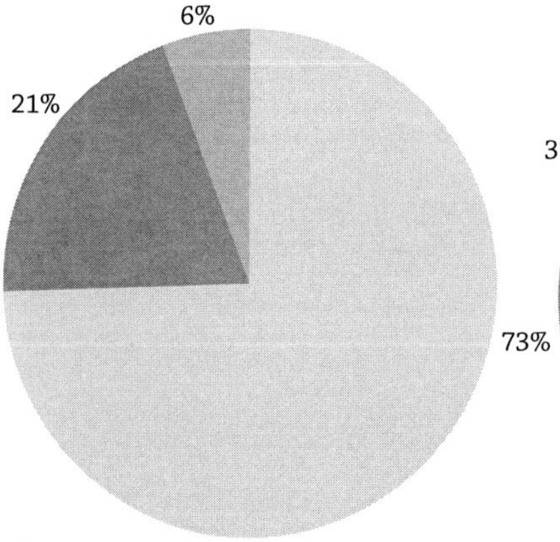

Figure 4.70(b)

Overall Satisfaction-Category B

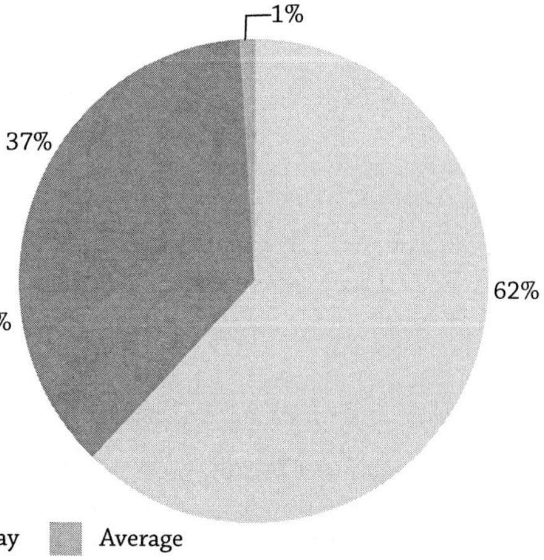

Number of Visits to Avail Services

Around 33 per cent of the citizens said that they visited the Mee Seva centres only once to get their work done, 31 per cent of them said that they visited twice, 18 per cent said that they had to visit three times, while 9 per cent and 9 per cent of them said that they visited four times or more than four times respectively, for getting their work done at Mee Seva centres.

Figure 4.71

No. of Visits to Avail Services

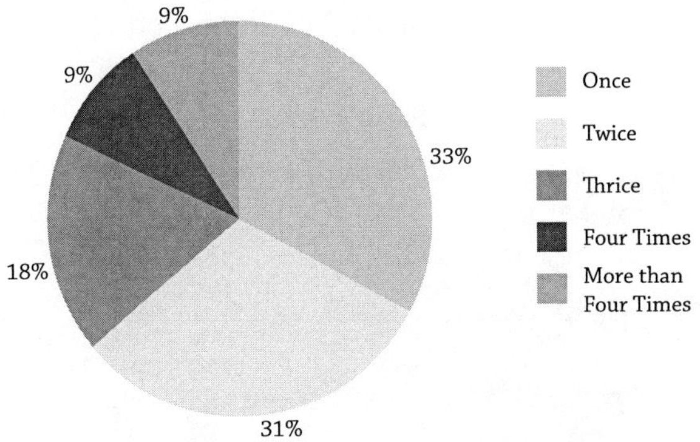

Paying Extra Money for Services

A question was raised on whether the citizens had to pay any extra money for accessing services from Mee Seva centres apart from the application fee. Around 98 per cent of the users who were contacted said that they did not pay any extra money to get their services from Mee Seva but around 2 per cent of the users said that they paid extra for accessing services from Mee Seva centres.

Figure 4.72

Paying Extra Money

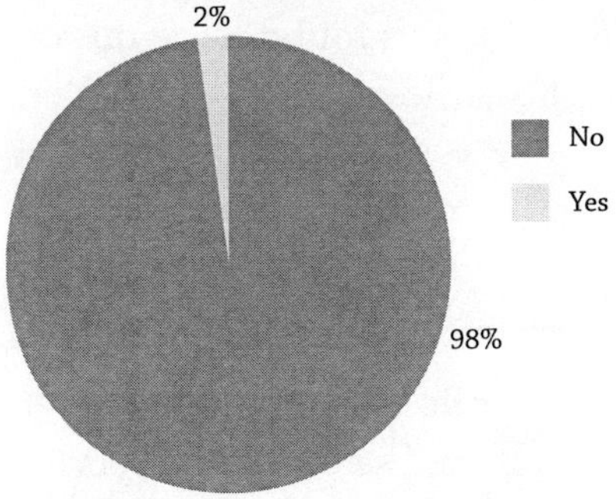

CSC Operators' View on the Reasons for Delay in Service Delivery

The CSC operators faced certain issues while delivering services to the citizens. The study found that 56 per cent of them faced a delay in the flow of information from the departments, 19 per cent stated that timelines were not adhered to, 13 per cent encountered

attitudinal issues, 7 per cent of them found a lack of interest in the Government towards the programme, and the remaining 5 per cent of them stated lack of clarity in the procedures that have been instituted.

Figure 4.73

CSC Operators View

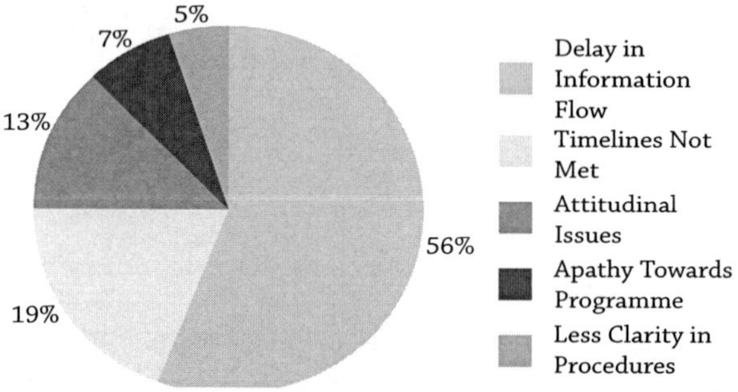

Observations by Field Teams

- The field team visiting Rangareddy district found that some CSCs were in crowded places, particularly near other government offices. The CSC operators were sometimes using the CSC infrastructure for offering other services which tend to impair the overall functioning of Mee Seva. The parking place in some CSCs was found to be missing which needs to be addressed at the earliest.

District: Srikakulam

Overall Satisfaction with Mee Seva Services

Under Category A Services [Figure 4.74(a)], around 86 per cent of the users who were contacted said that the services offered at the Mee Seva are good, 13 per cent of them felt that the service delivery at Mee Seva Centres is okay, while 1 per cent of them felt that the services at Mee Seva are average.

Under Category B Services [Figure 4.74(b)], around 80 per cent of the users who were contacted said that the services offered at Mee Seva are good, while 20 per cent of them said that the service delivery at Mee Seva centres is okay.

Figure 4.74(a)

Overall Satisfaction-Category A

Figure 4.74(b)

Overall Satisfaction-Category B

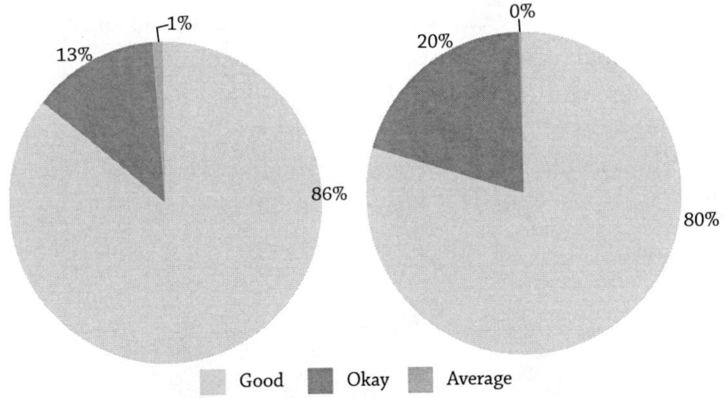

Number of Visits to Avail Services

Around 69 per cent of the citizens said that they visited the Mee Seva centres only once to get their work done, 25 per cent of them said that they visited twice, 3 per cent said that they visited three times, while 2 per cent and 1 per cent of them said that they visited four times or more than four times respectively, for getting their work done at Mee Seva centres.

Figure 4.75

No. of Visits to Avail Services

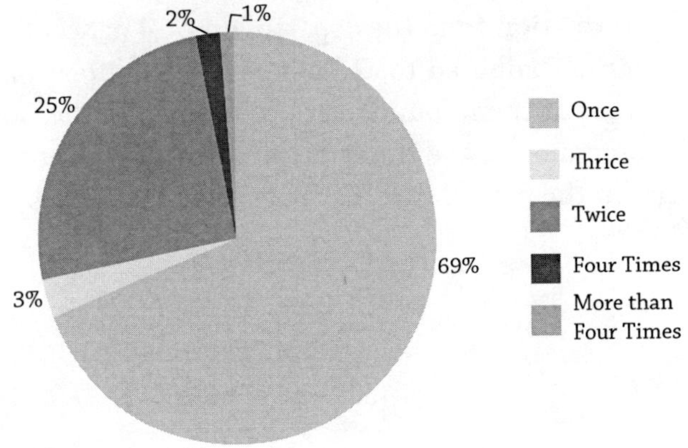

Paying Extra Money for Services

As a part of the survey, a question was raised on whether the citizens had to pay any extra money for accessing services from Mee Seva centres apart from the application fee. Around 94 per cent of the users who were contacted said that they did not pay any extra money to get their services from Mee Seva but around 6 per cent of the users said that they paid extra for accessing services from Mee Seva centres.

Figure 4.76

Paying Extra Money

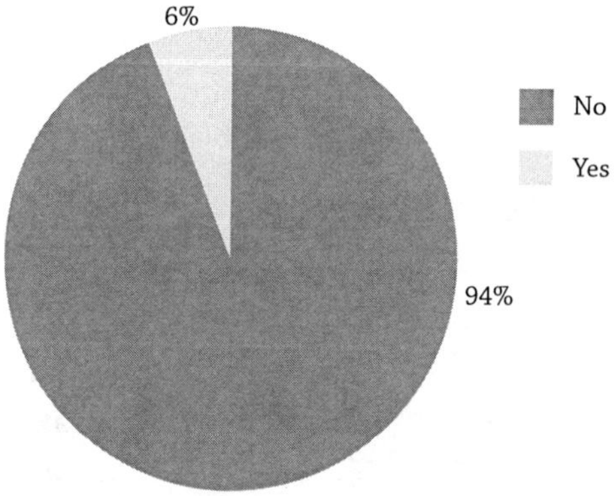

CSC Operators' View on the Reasons for Delay in Service Delivery

The CSC operators faced certain issues while delivering services to the citizens. The study found that 44 per cent of them faced a delay in the flow of information from the departments, 14 per cent stated that timelines were not adhered to, 20 per cent encountered attitudinal issues, 7 per cent of them found a lack of interest in the Government towards the programme, and the remaining 15 per cent of them stated lack of clarity in the procedures that have been instituted.

Figure 4.77

CSC Operators View

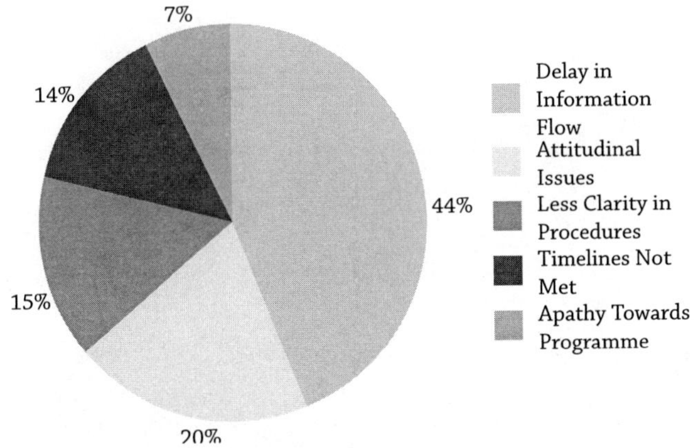

Observations by Field Teams

- The researchers found that there are instances of delay in service delivery and some villages are far from the centre. Besides, there is lack of awareness among people about the services available at the Mee Seva centres.
- Some centres are also providing services like photocopy, color prints, instantaneous passport size photos etc. The attitude of staff is very cooperative and polite.

District: Visakhapatnam

Overall Satisfaction with Mee Seva Services

Under Category A Services [Figure 4.78(a)], around 98 per cent of the users who were contacted said that the services offered at the Mee Seva are good, while 1 per cent of them felt that the service delivery at Mee Seva Centres is okay, while 1 per cent of them felt that the services at Mee Seva are average.

Under Category B Services [Figure 4.78(b)], around 91 per cent of the users who were contacted said that the services offered at Mee Seva are good, while 6 per cent of them said that the service delivery at Mee Seva centres is okay. Only 3 per cent of the users said that the service delivery by Mee Seva is average.

Figure 4.78(a)

Overall Satisfaction-Category A

Figure 4.78(b)

Overall Satisfaction-Category B

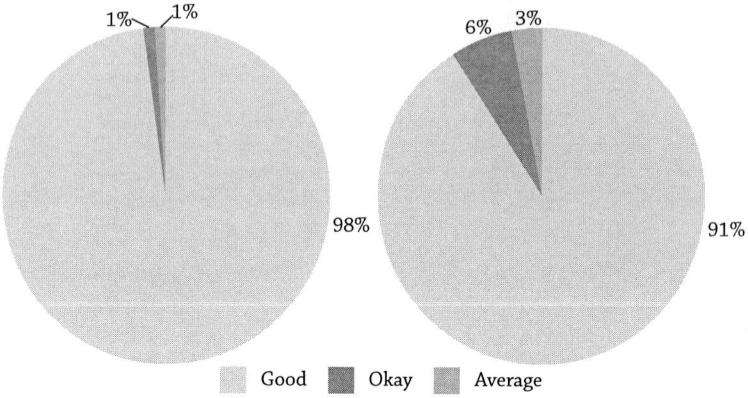

Number of Visits to Avail Services

Around 35 per cent of the citizens said that they visited only once to the Mee Seva centres to get their work done, while 32 per cent of them said that they visited twice and 12 per cent said that they visited three times, while 8 per cent and 13 per cent of them said that they visited four times or more than four times for getting their work done at Mee Seva centres.

Figure 4.79

No. of Visits to Avail Services

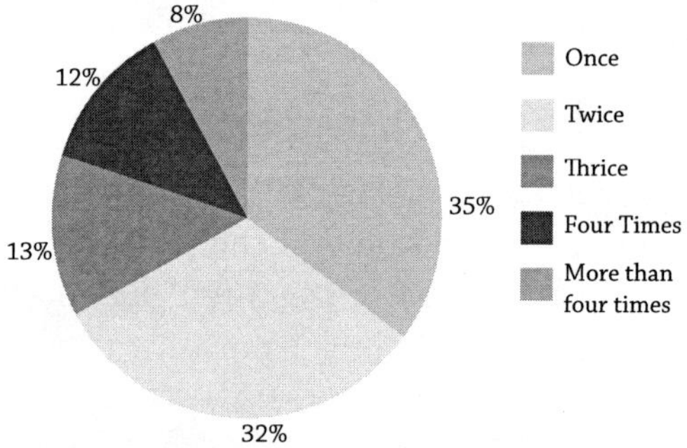

Paying Extra Money for Services

A question was raised on whether the citizens had to pay any extra money for accessing services from Mee Seva Centres apart from the application fee. Around 99 per cent of the users who were contacted said that they did not pay any extra money to get their services from Mee Seva and around 1 per cent of the users said that they paid money for accessing services from Mee Seva centres.

Figure 4.80

Paying Extra Money

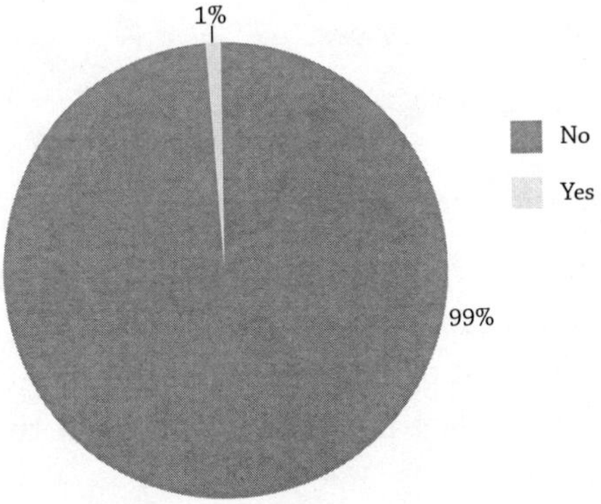

CSC Operators' View on the Reasons for Delay in Service Delivery

The CSC operators faced certain issues while delivering services to the citizens. The study found that 35 per cent of them faced a delay in the flow of information from the departments, 16 per cent stated that timelines were not adhered to, 18 per cent encountered attitudinal issues, 8 per cent of them found a lack of interest in the Government towards the programme, and the remaining 8 per cent of them stated lack of clarity in the procedures that have been instituted.

Figure 4.81

CSC Operators' View

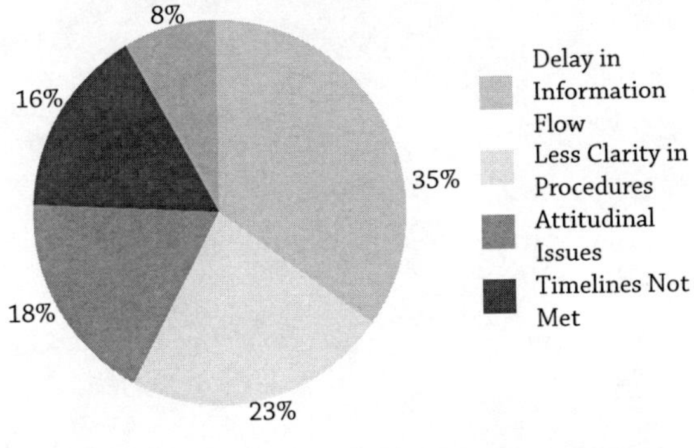

Observations by Field Teams

- The researchers found that some centres did not have ample space for the staff to perform their duties, and there were no basic facilities including lights, fans and drinking water available at the centre. Slow network connectivity hampered speedy delivery of services.

District: Vizianagaram

Overall Satisfaction with Mee Seva Services

Under Category A Services [Figure 4.82(a)], around 71 per cent of the users who were contacted said that the services offered at the Mee Seva are good, 28 per cent of them felt that the service delivery at Mee Seva centres is okay, while 1 per cent of them felt that the services at Mee Seva are average.

Under Category B Services [Figure 4.82(b)], around 83 per cent of the users who were contacted said that the services offered at Mee Seva are good, while 16 per cent of them said that the service delivery at Mee Seva centres is okay. Only 1 per cent of the users said that the service delivery by Mee Seva is average.

Figure 4.82(a)

Overall Satisfaction-Category A

Figure 4.82(b)

Overall Satisfaction-Category B

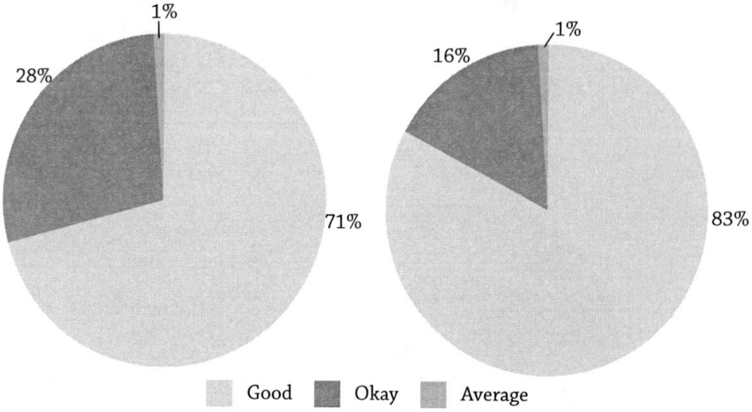

Number of Visits to Avail Services

Around 59 per cent of the citizens said that they visited the Mee Seva centres only once to get their work done, while 39 per cent of them said that they visited twice, 2 per cent said that they visited three times for getting their work done at Mee Seva centres.

Figure 4.83

No. of Visits to Avail Services

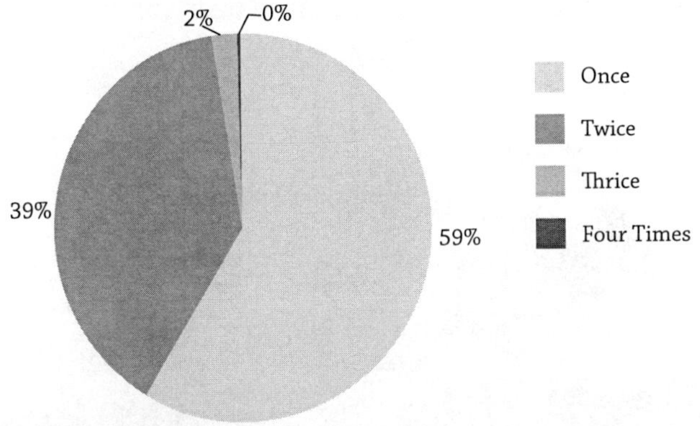

Paying Extra Money for Services

A question was raised on whether the citizens had to pay any extra money for accessing services from Mee Seva centres apart from the application fee. Around 95 per cent of the users who were contacted said that they did not pay any extra money to get their services from Mee Seva but around 5 per cent of the users said that they paid extra for accessing services from Mee Seva centres.

Figure 4.84

Paying Extra Money

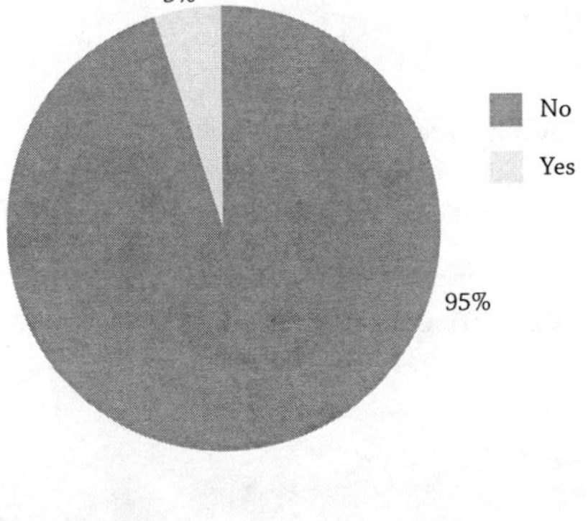

CSC Operators' View on the Reasons for Delay in Service Delivery

The CSC operators faced certain issues while delivering services to the citizens. The study found that 43 per cent of them faced a delay in the flow of information from the departments, 14 per cent stated that timelines were not adhered to, 18 per cent encountered attitudinal issues, 12 per cent of them found a lack of interest in the Government towards the programme, and the remaining 13 per cent of them stated lack of clarity in the procedures that have been instituted.

Figure 4.85

CSC Operators View

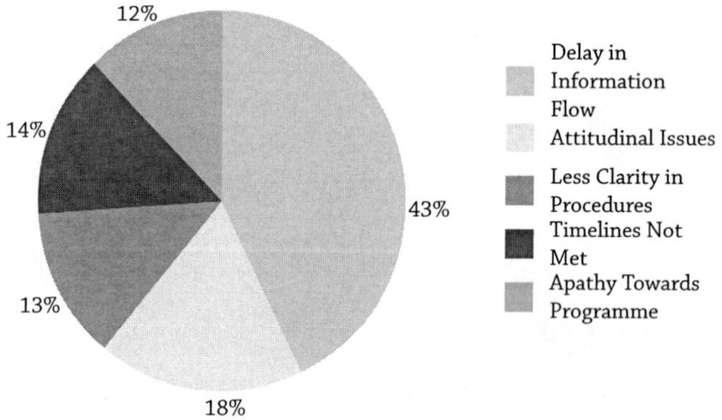

Observations by Field Teams

- The field team found that the CSCs are not well equipped and the power supply was erratic creating dissatisfaction among the citizens. Some CSCs did not have adequate number of chairs for the people. The quality of the printers too needs to be up graded as the printing quality was not good.

District: Warangal

Overall Satisfaction with Mee Seva Services

Under Category A Services [Figure 4.86(a)], around 39 per cent of the users who were contacted said that the services offered at the Mee Seva are good, 60 per cent of them felt that the service delivery at Mee

Seva Centres is okay, while 1 per cent of them felt that the services at Mee Seva are average.

Under Category B Services [Figure 4.86(b)], around 31 per cent of the users who were contacted said that the services offered at Mee Seva are good, while 67 per cent of them said that the service delivery at Mee Seva centres is okay. Only 2 per cent of the users said that the service delivery by Mee Seva is average.

Figure 4.86(a)

Overall Satisfaction-Category A

Figure 4.86(b)

Overall Satisfaction-Category B

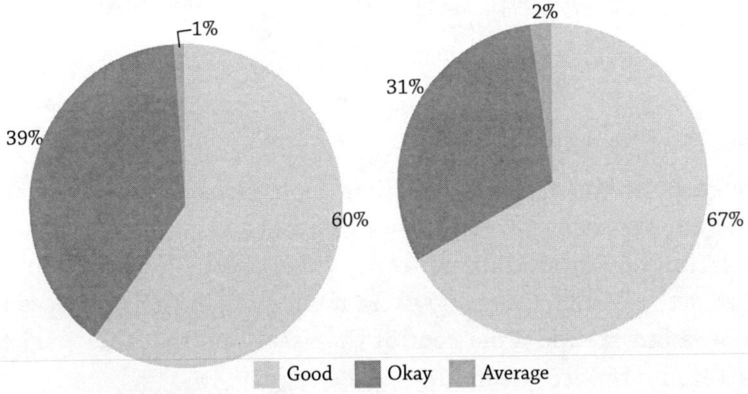

Number of Visits to Avail Services

Around 38 per cent of the citizens said that they visited the Mee Seva centres only once to get their work done, 42 per cent of them said that they visited twice, 11 per cent said that they visited three times, while 3 per cent and 6 per cent of them said that they visited four times or more than four times respectively, for getting their work done at Mee Seva centres.

Figure 4.87

No. of Visits to Avail Services

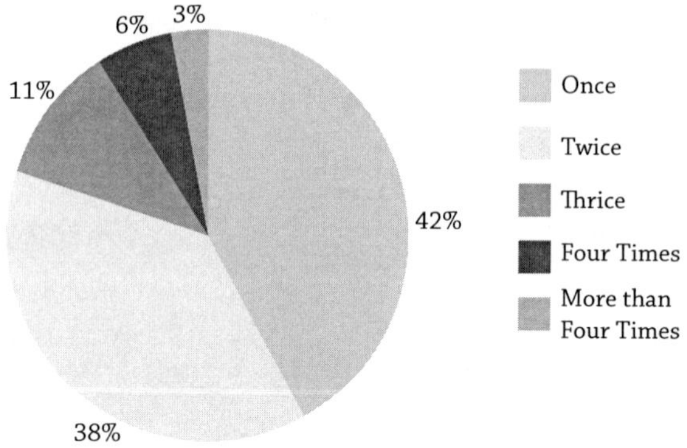

Paying Extra Money for Services

A question was raised on whether the citizens had to pay any extra money for accessing services from Mee Seva centres apart from the application fee. Around 98 per cent of the users who were contacted said that they did not pay any extra money to get their services from Mee Seva but around 2 per cent of the users said that they paid extra for accessing services from Mee Seva centres.

Figure 4.88

Paying Extra Money

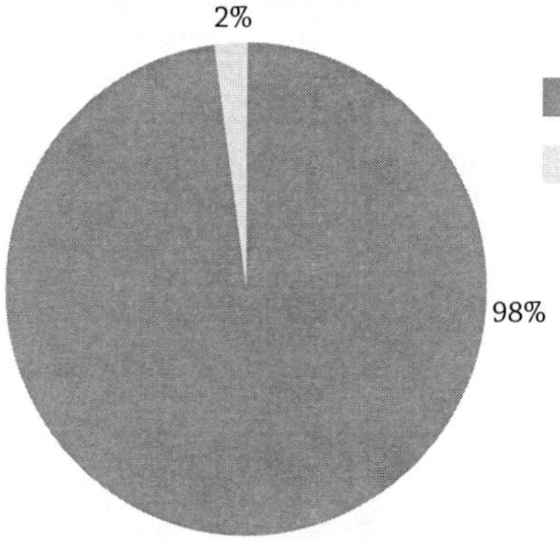

CSC Operators' View on the Reasons for Delay in Service Delivery

The CSC operators faced certain issues while delivering services to the citizens. The study found that 52 per cent of them faced a delay in the flow of information from the departments, 7 per cent stated that timelines were not adhered to, 22 per cent encountered attitudinal issues, 10 per cent of them found a lack of interest in the Government towards the programme, and the remaining 9 per cent of them stated lack of clarity in the procedures that have been instituted.

Figure 4.89

CSC Operators' View

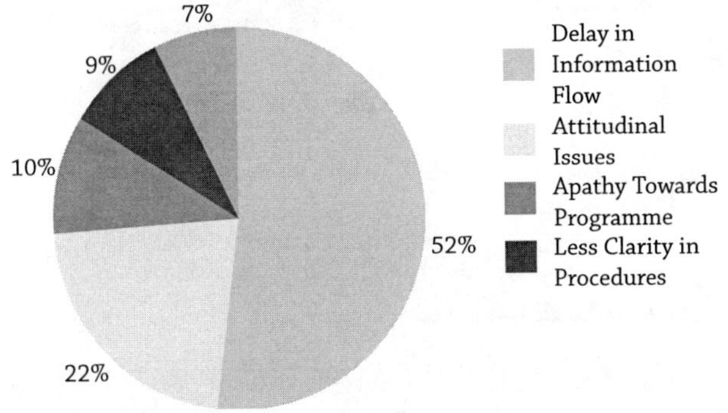

Observations by Field Teams

- The CSCs which were visited by the field team were found to be in good shape—good number of chairs, display of the Mee Seva charter, etc. However, the CSCs in rural areas were small in size and were simple in outlook, but were providing good services to the citizens. The research team interacted with citizens and found that they were happy with the Mee Seva services.

District: West Godavari

Overall Satisfaction with Mee Seva Services

Under Category A Services [Figure 4.90(a)], around 55 per cent of the users who were contacted said that the services offered at the Mee Seva are good, 42 per cent of them felt that the service delivery at Mee Seva Centres is okay, while 3 per cent of them felt that the services at Mee Seva are average.

Under Category B Services [Figure 4.90(b)], around 63 per cent of the users who were contacted said that the services offered at Mee Seva are good, while 35 per cent of them said that the service delivery at Mee Seva centres is okay. Only 2 per cent of the users said that the service delivery by Mee Seva is average.

Figure 4.90(a)

Overall Satisfaction-Category A

Figure 4.90(b)

Overall Satisfaction-Category B

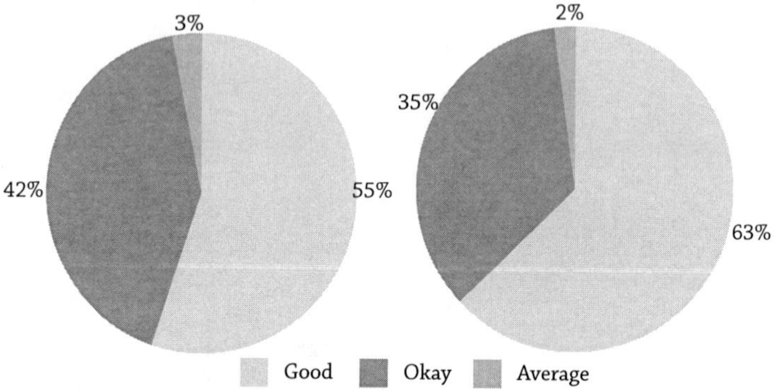

Number of Visits to Avail Services

Around 49 per cent of the citizens said that they visited the Mee Seva centres only once to get their work done, 24 per cent of them said that they visited twice, 8 per cent said that they visited three times, while 6 per cent and 13 per cent of them said that they visited four times or more than four times respectively, for getting their work done at Mee Seva centres.

Figure 4.91

No. of Visits to Avail Services

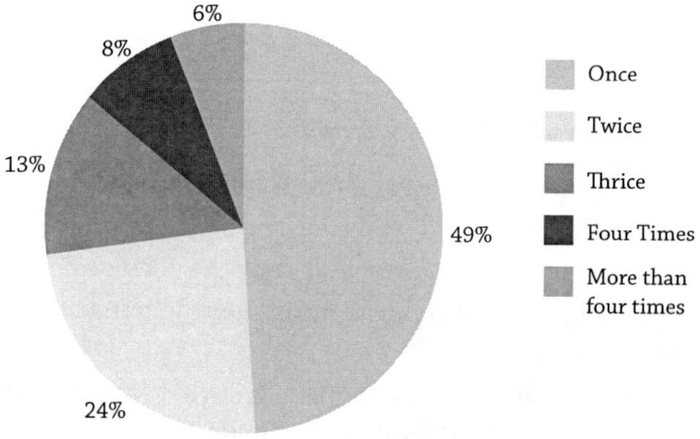

Paying Extra Money for Services

As a part of the survey, a question was raised on whether the citizens had to pay any extra money for accessing services from Mee Seva Centres apart from the application fee. Around 98 per cent of the users who were contacted said that they did not pay any extra money to get their services from Mee Seva but around 2 per cent of the users said that they paid extra for accessing services from Mee Seva centres.

Figure 4.92

Paying Extra Money

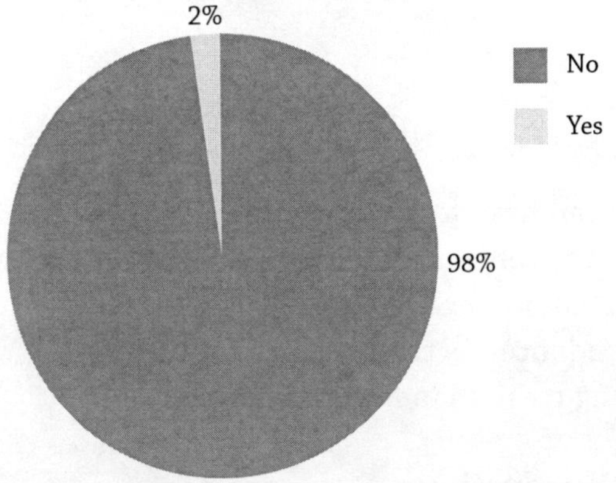

CSC Operators' View on the Reasons for Delay in Service Delivery

The CSC operators faced certain issues while delivering services to the citizens. The study found that 51 per cent of them faced a delay in the flow of information from the departments, 12 per cent stated that timelines were not adhered to, 21 per cent encountered attitudinal issues, 9 per cent of them found a lack of interest in the Government towards the programme, and the remaining 7 per cent of them stated lack of clarity in the procedures that have been instituted.

Figure 4.93

CSC Operators' View

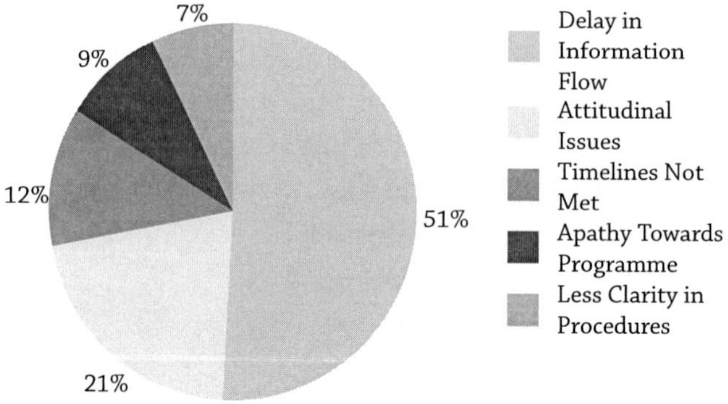

Observations by Field Teams

- The researchers found that due to power failure, people are visiting the centres more than twice to get their work done, but there is no delay on account of the staff. For some certificates like Residence Certificate, Income Certificate, etc., people are travelling more than five kilometres.

Concluding Observations

Given the high satisfaction levels of the citizens regarding Mee Seva, there is a need to strengthen its performance and streamline the processes further. Mee Seva is found to be an effective tool to curb delay in the delivery of citizen services and the data point to the fact that the citizens are happy with this model of public service delivery. One should not forget the fact that the integration of the technology with the back-end processes has led to a dramatic change in the public service delivery marked with timeliness, quality, accountability, responsibility and citizen satisfaction.

The corruption issues wherein the citizens are forced to shell out money for availing services too have been minimised as the respondents in most of the cases have stated that they did not pay money to avail the services. The CSCs which act as intermediaries for providing the services have successfully acted as firewalls between the government departments and the citizens, thereby reducing the scope for corrupt practices.

There are still certain glitches which need to be addressed—lack of necessary infrastructure, erratic power supply, lack of good printers, internet connectivity problems, mistakes in data bank provided by the government departments, etc. However, looking at the larger picture of e-governance and the initiatives taken to simplify the public service delivery, the functioning of Mee Seva can be considered as path breaking. The ease and simplicity with which the services are provided are indicative of good governance and better public service delivery.

5

Stakeholder Discussions

In an attempt to understand different dimensions of the functioning of Mee Seva, an attempt was made to elicit the views of the departments involved in the delivery of services. As a part of the stakeholder discussion, the Institute of Public Enterprises (IPE) team met officials from revenue and registration departments to know their views on Mee Seva implementation. Discussions were held with the following stakeholders from the Revenue department from 29 October 2012 till 31 October 2012:

- Deputy Collectors.
- *Tahsildars*.
- Mandal Revenue Inspectors.
- Village Revenue Offices (VROs).

Discussions were held with district registrars and senior officials from the Registration and Stamps Department, Government of Andhra Pradesh.

Registration Department

The Registration Department initiated the process of computerisation of records in 1983. Hence, the department has data for almost 30 years.

As a part of the Mee Seva service in the year 2012, the Registration Department is offering the following two services:

- Encumbrance Certificate.
- Certified copies.

As per the vision of the Government of Andhra Pradesh (GoAP), computerising documents regarding these key services by the department will simplify the work and end office drudgery that the employees endure. This will make things easier for citizens. It is also felt that employees of the department will have more time to put their house in order.

The department is confronting certain issues. Currently in 12 districts, services of Encumberance Certificate and Certified copies have been stopped from the Sub-Registrar and all these certificates are being issued only through Mee Seva. The districts are: Vijaynagaram, Krishna, Nellore, Khammam, Karimnagar, Mahbubnagar, Nizamabad, Nalgonda, Medak, Rangareddy, Hyderabad and Chittoor.

The key issues which came up during discussions include:

- *Software issues:* the CARD software has been developed by National Informatics Centre (NIC), and Mee Seva software has been developed by APOnline. There were few issues initially which have now been addressed successfully. As of now there are no issues with regards to the software.
- *Skill and knowledge levels of Data Centre Operators (DCOs):* during the interaction with customers, the study found that skill levels of the operators working at the Mee Seva counters are thought to be slightly lacking. During some transactions, it was found that inputting details were incorrect. This caused few problems in getting the right information from the sub-registrar's office and consequently, the whole process of service delivery was delayed. The level of knowledge of the operator initially hindered the efficient service delivery. The ICT Department has attended to this issue by encouraging capacity building measures amongst operators.
- *Printing quality:* the printing quality is one of the major issues plaguing these services. The Department has consistently received complaints on the printing quality of the document. The documents are printed by the centre operators in such a manner that most of the time they are not useful for the purpose for which it was taken. Citizens have to visit the department to get the documents they require. The ICT Department took corrective steps and the printing of the certificates is found to be good now.

- *Monitoring:* the roles assigned to the departmental officials were not clear enough to monitor the project. Necessary instructions have been given to the people involved in the implementation of Mee Seva to provide handholding support to the field offices for effective execution of the entire project. The Registration Department need not monitor Mee Seva as common service centres. Joint Collector at the district level monitors the progress from time to time.
- *Training HRD:* training and capacity building of the district and field offices of the department has been conducted a number of times for bringing about greater clarity among the employees about their roles and responsibilities as a part of the project. Conducting training for the district and field offices should be further encouraged as the stakeholders have been sensitised towards change. Training programmes have been found to make the stakeholders ready for accepting and initiating change in the department.
- *Mindset issues:* the programme is expected to curb delays and benefit citizens. Therefore, it means dealing with the mindset of employees who have been at the forefront of the delivery of services. This may include making them understand that their role in the delivery of services is of utmost importance in strengthening Mee Seva.

  Some employees found that Mee Seva has not reduced drudgery from their job. In fact, throughout the day one person has to sit before the computer and wait for application details to arrive. This does not ease matters for them. However, probing the issue further has led to the finding that the employees need not sit before the computer throughout the day. They are expected to log on at periodic intervals and find out the number of applications.

  As the delivery of services is being expanded through electronic mode, programmes that assist in dealing with changing need to be administered by the officers at various levels. This will help in addressing the mindset issues. That apart, mindset issues can be better addressed through continuous support from senior officers at all levels.

Revenue Department

The process of streamlining service delivery in the Revenue Department started long before Mee Seva was established. Computerisation of land records started sometime in the year 2003. This led to the setting up of Bhoomi counters, around the year 2009-10, where citizens got their services in stipulated timelines and without much difficulty.

A lot of preparatory activity occurred before this service was actually launched. The Revenue Department did a lot of process review in terms of identifying services that could be provided to citizens through Mee Seva. Developing a common database was another major initiative taken by the department. For example, the development of a student database was the first attempt made by the government towards creating a centralised database.

Some of implementation issues that came in for discussion have been put forth in the subsequent sections. The focus has been to understand administrative and managerial issues at the field level, and partially touch upon the technical aspects involved.

In terms of the institutional arrangements for implementing Mee Seva programme, the structural arrangements that have been put in place at the district level include the Joint Collector and Special Deputy Collector who are responsible for looking after the Mee Seva subject/issues. At the *Tahsil* level, the *Tahsildar* is responsible for the implementation of Mee Seva.

Offering Mee Seva is a highly specialised initiative and therefore there is a need for specialised technical support at various levels of implementation. This has been provided in terms of a District Information Officer (NIC resource), Mee Seva Handholding resource person, Institute of Electronic Governance (resource person) at the district level. At the divisional level, there are handholding persons who assist the departments in implementation of the programme.

At the sub-divisional level, there are operators who provided minimal technical support for Mee Seva.

Basic training at the field level was given by the NIC to the implementing departments before the launch of the Mee Seva project. Connectivity was provided by the Government to the department for providing services.

Regular reports regarding the application received, disposed and pending for various services were sent to all the concerned officials on a daily basis.

Well performing districts have been given awards and recognised for their good work. Despite all the efforts, there are certain key issues that need to be addressed to make the Mee Seva service more effective and efficient.

Key Issues

- *Workload:* officials at various levels right from the district level to divisional and sub-divisional levels have been assigned responsibilities for implementing Mee Seva. These responsibilities are considered to be additional roles that the officials are performing. However, in practical terms the Mee Seva work is not an additional work as it only a change in the mode of functioning—manual to technological.
- *Roles and responsibilities:* fixing roles and responsibilities at various levels is very important. For instance, before Mee Seva the certified copies were being signed by Deputy *Tahsildar* and certificates were signed by *Tahsildar*. With Mee Seva in force, the *Tahsildars* are responsible for signing both categories of documents, and they hold the master key for digital signatures. Due to multiple roles, they are not able to take the support of anyone in this activity and this causes a delay in the delivery of service in some instances.
- *Data correctness:* implementation of Mee Seva requires a lot of preparatory work to be done in terms of record keeping, computerisation of data, verification of data etc., so that certificates can be given within a short time as specified in

the charter. In the case of Revenue Department, the process of development of student database was attempted and all the data was put together. But during implementation, it was found that the data received from schools was not present in an appropriate manner. Problems like mismatch of information, problems in verification, duplication etc., were cropping up. Inaccuracy of data hampered the department's ability to provide services within the specified timelines and to overcome such a problem, efforts were made to authenticate the date with field visits. There could have been some cases of duplication and inaccuracy. However, apart from that, the databases have been streamlined. The issues of discrepancy are not regular and may occasionally crop up in certain areas.

- *Time management:* the *Tahsildar*, who is responsible for multiple issues in the field level has less time to sit in front of the computer to wait for an application to arrive and then endorse it. Therefore, meeting timelines is a serious issue. The *Tahsildar* need not sit before the computer throughout the day. Rather, he or she may look for applications at regular intervals—twice or thrice a day.
- *Technical support:* technical support in the form of handholding support that must be made available at the divisional level is actually not present at the *Tahsildars* office. Thus, the key person responsible for implementing the scheme at the field is handicapped due to the lack of technical support. The technical team has been strengthened now because the issues have been addressed by the ICT Department.
- *Budget:* there is no budget that has been allocated by the Government for the implementation of Mee Seva. The preparatory activities involve computerisation, scanning of data and uploading of data. Due to a dearth of money, the officials are unable to hire the services of technical persons to get the data computerised and upload data. Data entry operators have now been provided in the offices to ensure that the data entry is done properly and on time.

- *Reporting:* in some divisions, there was no proper flow of information from the sub-divisional level to divisional level to the district level. *Tahsildar* assigned RIs (Revenue Inspectors) and VROs to look after the service centres, but they did not have an idea of the day-to-day occurrences of the centre, issues and problems of the people and so on. These are stray cases and such cases are being monitored through daily reports.
- *Monitoring:* monitoring was missing in the implementation of the project. When asked about the frequency of monitoring of Mee Seva activity, the officials were unable to explain anything. Some of them said that during the monthly review with the collector, these issues are discussed and reviewed. However, no daily reviews, weekly reviews and monthly reviews are being done by the Special Deputy Collectors who are responsible for the implementation of Mee Seva. The Joint Collector takes stock of the situation now and thus there is no need to keep a tab everyday and every hour, and as the data shows that the citizens are happy with the services, therefore no need for micro management.
- *Grievance redressal:* grievance redressal was also an issue. There are various levels at which the grievances are expected to be redressed as per the charter. In the process of implementation, it was found that there were no clear timelines indicated for disposal of grievances and issues of various levels including the top levels. Each service has now been given a clear timeframe and it is found that services are being provided on time. However, there can be some astray cases where the timelines might not have been met. Such cases are negligible.
- *Timeliness:* in specific service (as in the case of Family Member Certificate), the timeline indicated in the Charter is 7-15 days, but it is not sufficient. Therefore, timelines need to be reviewed so that service standards are met. For a service to be provided, a fortnight is sufficient and reasonable; taking more time than that may be against the spirit of Mee Seva.

- *Multiple agencies:* there are multiple agencies at the field level which have established Mee Seva centres, such as they are APOnline, CMS, Sreeven, Spanco, etc.

Inputs from VROs and Revenue Inspectors

- *Training for operators:* Mee Seva operators were not provided sufficient training in uploading the necessary documents for different services and therefore, they were not able to upload all the required and necessary documents while sending the application form to the *Tahsildar* office. This led to a piling up of applications and a delay in service delivery. The study found that the operators have now been trained sufficiently to handle the applications. This apart, a checklist is provided which ensures that each application, based on the nature of the service, is supported by relevant documents.
- *Training for officers:* The capacity building programmes need to be organised for VROs; also as they enable them to understand the latest developments in various services. This is particularly true with regards to computer knowledge; once they are stuck with an issue on the computer, they are not able to move forward, leading to delay. The Service Centre Agencies (SCA) should be given the responsibility to train the VROs as well. This practice will go a long way in delivering the services more efficiently. The VROs are meant for checking the information at the field level and not for providing services to citizens. They inspect the field data submitted by the citizens and send the verifying report to the *Tahsildar*. They do not need computer training with regard to delivery of services of Mee Seva.
- *Time constraints:* The revenue officers are not able to devote much time to field inquiry for providing various services which also lead to an increase in the number of SLA (service-level agreement) cases. The field inquiry is not a new role that has been taken up by the revenue officials. What has changed is the time bound format of Mee Seva services which might have led them to face time constraints.

- *Dependence on outsourced employees:* There is high dependence of revenue officers on outsourced employees whose attendance and commitment levels are not that appreciable. As the entire format is designed that way, dependence on outsourced employees cannot be avoided. The issue of addressing the problems arising from the outsourced employees is left for the concerned *Tahsildars*.
- *Correctness of land records:* There were many instances where the land records of the revenue department were not getting tallied resulting in delay in cross-verification, and thus delaying the final service for citizens. Digitisation of all the records has been completed and such problems will not arise in the future.

Conclusion

The various issues discussed in the chapter highlight how Mee Seva has certain constraints to overcome so as to become more effective in the delivery of better services to the citizens. There are certain systemic issues, beyond the control of Mee Seva like incorrect name of the citizens, wrong addresses, etc., which need to be addressed by the Revenue Department at the earliest. That apart, there are certain issues like dependence on outsource employees to get the work done, which can be addressed by the officers concerned, rather than highlighting them as major problems. The study shows that there are certain issues with regard to addressing the grievances of the citizens in case of wrong entry on the certificate, repeated visits to Mee Seva to get the services, quality of certificate paper, etc., all of which can be suitably addressed by the ICT Department of the Government. In most of the cases, as the study has shown, the timelines are being adhered to by Mee Seva and sufficient proof was found with the researchers that the citizens are highly satisfied with the one-stop-shop for government services, located in accessible parts of the state.

6

Conclusions and Suggestions

After studying the various aspects of Mee Seva implementation, and interacting with both the demand side and the supply side, there were a couple of issues that emerged in terms of implementation of Mee Seva project.

The Mee Seva programme in Andhra Pradesh (AP) is one of the flagship programmes conceived by the Government. There is a vision behind this project and if successfully implemented, it will transform governance and service delivery in AP. Some issues that have cropped up during the study are discussed below.

Fine Tuning the Service Delivery

The study found that across the state certain certificates are not being issued to citizens on time and this is being perceived negatively by the respondents. The districts in which the service of Other Backward Classes (OBC) Certificate was perceived negatively are Nizamabad and Medak. Krishna district was lacking in the issuance of the Integrated Certificate within specified time frame.

In the case of services like Integrated Certificate, as a preparatory step student data is collected in advance. However, when it comes to implementation through Mee Seva, there are certain inaccuracies which lead to revenue officials wasting time over verification and thus lengthening the process.

The study found that in those departments which provide the bulk of services to the citizens, most of the activities have been streamlined and the officers of such departments are carrying out the tasks well. This apart, the officers who are responsible for all the activities have been sensitised and trained sufficiently so that they deliver the services properly. With high citizen satisfaction, it can be stated that Mee Seva has been received well by the citizens. In case the

ICT Department finds any improvement in the service delivery, it may contact the respective departments and do the needful.

Adhering to Service Delivery Timelines

The study found that in some cases, the respondents get services the very first instance; in other cases they are made to visit the centres again and again. For example, in the case of corrections in Adangal/ Pahani, the respondents in the districts of Warangal, Cuddapah, Rangareddy, Nellore, Visakhapatnam and West Godavari had to visit Mee Seva centres four or more times. In the case of FMB Copy too, the users had to visit centres number of time especially in the districts of West Godavari, Nizamabad, Visakhapatnam, Prakasam, Cuddapah and Nellore. Similar experiences have been shared by respondents with regard to No Earning Certificate in the districts of Warangal, Visakhapatnam, Cuddapah, Anantapur, Prakasam and Karimnagar.

The focus of Mee Seva is to provide timely services to the citizens and ensure that they need not visit the centres multiple times to avail the service. The reasons for the delay in the delivery of the services should be found and corrective actions must be taken. The mails which are received by PMU (Project Monitoring Unit) and the calls received through toll free number 1100 should be attended immediately to make corrective actions. These actions are likely to make the delivery of services to the citizens faster under Mee Seva.

Functional Clarity

Government orders have been issued to clarify the field level roles. For instance, the Special Deputy Collector at the district level and *Tahsiladar* at the *Taluka* level have been assigned to monitor the implementation of the project. During discussions, the officials clearly stated that due to other job responsibilities they were not able to put in all their energies in monitoring implementation. In case the role of the Special Deputy Collector is not specifically designed to monitor the implementation of Mee Seva, the government may ponder over the issue and assign an officer exclusively for monitoring Mee Seva implementation at the district level. If that had been already done, there is no need to tinker with the system.

Coordination and Convergence

There are a number of departments involved in the implementation of Mee Seva. It has been observed that coordination and convergence among various departments at the state level, district level, divisional level and sub-divisional level can be improvised upon. A Coordination Committee comprising members from the key departments in each district may be set up for ensuring better coordination in the implementation of Mee Seva. The same may be headed by the Joint Collector at the district level.

Monitoring

There is a need for physical verifications, inspections and checks to keep the system running efficiently. Particularly, the officials of the ICT Department may play an important role in monitoring the implementation of Mee Seva services from time to time.

Strengthening Infrastructure

Strengthening the infrastructure in their offices will improve the efficiency of service delivery in the state. The CSCs need to have adequate space, systems, power backups and other such things. Power failure has been a major constraint in the delivery of the services to the citizens and unless this is improved, CSCs may suffer in their work. Hence, they can be asked to invest in inverters with longer backup so that the services to the citizens are not interfered.

Mindset Issues

Another aspect in Mee Seva implementation is the mindset issues of the officials involved in the delivery of services. It has been found that there is a slight resistance towards this programme. This may not be an ideal situation for the success of the project. One factor is that all along, the officers have been doing field work and have been interacting with people in the delivery of the services. Introduction of Mee Seva changed their role and their new role is not to their liking. Any change management programme will have such issues but these problems can be tackled through different methods. With Mee Seva getting firmly entrenched all over the state, it can be stated that more or less, most officials have accepted the way services are delivered to the citizens. In case the ICT Department continues to encounter such issues, it may give awards to those officials who have done well in the delivery of services. Such awards can have demonstration effect and over a period of time, more officials may start exhibiting interest towards Mee Seva.

Capacity Building

There are certain issues with operators like entering wrong information which lead to delays and causes dissatisfaction among citizens. During interactions with senior officials also, this problem was presented as a major factor for delay in service delivery. There is a need to identify skilled personnel at CSCs. From time to time, the operators need to be sensitised and trained so that they understand how accurate data entry is crucial for the delivery of services. The operators must also be well equipped to assist citizens in filling up forms as most of the time those who come to avail services don't have experience of filling up forms and need help.

Curbing Corrupt Practices

Mee Seva takes away the human interface in service delivery making it more difficult to indulge in rent-seeking. As per the service charter, there is a standard user fee and no extra amount should be paid by the citizens to avail the services. In most cases citizens stated that they did not pay extra money to avail the services. Although, some extra payment of money was reported in some cases. However, with more awareness among citizens, the problem is expected to come down. Display boards may play an important role as they provide details of the user fee for each service. If citizens are sensitised about malafide practices more often, there is a possibility these can be curbed over a period of time.

References

Government of Andhra Pradesh (2000). *A Module of Reform Initiatives in Administration.* Developed by MCR HRD IAP.

———. (2005). *Governance Reforms and Public Management Strategy.* Hyderabad: Centre for Good Governance.

———. (2011). *Andhra Pradesh Information Technology (Electronic Service Delivery) Rules.* Information Technology and Communications Department.

National eGovernance Plan (2009). *National eGovernance Plan Overview: NeGP Round Table.* July 29.

Planning Commission (2001). *Approach Paper to Tenth Five Year Plan (2002-2007).* New Delhi: Government of India.

———. (2004). *India Vision 2020: A Report.* New Delhi: Government of India.

———. (2011). *Faster, Sustainable, and More Inclusive Growth: An Approach to the Twelfth Five Year Plan.* New Delhi: Government of India.

Memos:

Government of Andhra Pradesh, Information Technology and Communications Department, G.O.Rt. No.1, dated 3.1.2012.

Government of Andhra Pradesh, Information Technology and Communications Department, G.O.Ms.No 4, dated 1.3.2012.

Government of Andhra Pradesh, Information Technology and Communications Department, Lr. No. 05/Mee Seva/Secy/IT&C/2012, dated 5.3.2012

Annexure

Format for Discussion with Heads of Participating Departments

Name of the Department:		*Name of the Official:*
Designation:	*Location:*	*Date of Survey:*

1. Please share with us the preparatory activities your department has undertaken for participating in the Mee Seva Service delivery:

   Supply Side:

   a. Internal process review
   b. Identifying accountability nodes
   c. Developing citizens charters
   d. Dealing with the mindset issues
   e. Any others

   Demand Side:

   f. Awareness programmes conducted
   g. Grievance redressal

2. Please discuss the convergence and coordination issues you face in terms of implementation of this programme:

   a. At the state level: inter departmental
   b. At the district level
   c. With the CSC owners and operators
   d. Any other issues

3. Kindly share with us the issues you face in terms of monitoring the field level implementation:

   a. Flow of information
   b. Checks
   c. Inspections
   d. Reporting and frequency
   e. Handholding
   f. Incentives and disincentives

Questionnaire for CSC Operators at Mee Seva Services

Name of the District: *Service Centre Code:*

I. *Personal Information:*

1. Name : ______________________________
2. Age: ______________
3. *Educational Qualifications:*
    a. SSC
    b. Intermediate
    c. Graduate
    d. Post Graduate and above

II. Training & Sensitisation

4. Did you receive training for taking up the job of a CSC operator? (if no, go to Q 10)
    a. Yes
    b. No
5. How many times did you receive training on Mee Seva?
    a. Once
    b. Twice
    c. Thrice
    d. More than thrice
6. Who gave you training?
    a. Government
    b. Service Centre Agency
    c. Others
7. Do you think the training you received is sufficient for you to discharge your duties effectively?
    a. Yes
    b. No
8. If no, what should be the frequency of training and sensitization to the operating staff at the Mee Seva centre?
    a. Once in 3 months
    b. Once in 6 months
    c. Once in a year

9. In which areas (like registration services, revenue services, general computer application, or anything else) would you like to get trained?

   Ans. ____

III. *Citizen Interface Issues:*

9. What are your responsibilities, when a citizen comes to the Mee Seva centre? (Multiple answering allowed and question will be asked as an open-ended question)
   a. Give them the application form
   b. Explain them about the documents to be submitted for the service they require
   c. Help them in filling application
   d. Process the application
   e. Help them locate status of the application
   f. Direct them towards grievance redressal
   g. Any other__________

IV. *Coordination Issues*

10. What are the issues you face in terms of dealing with the departments for accessing information?
    a. Delay in information flow from the respective departments
    b. Lack of clarity in the laid down procedures
    c. Timelines indicated in the Citizens Charters are not met with
    d. Lack of interest towards this programme
    e. Attitudinal issues
11. How do you rate technical support from SCA?
    a. Very good
    b. Good
    c. Poor

V. *Impressions*

12. What is your impression about the usefulness of Mee Seva centre for the citizen?
    a. Very useful
    b. Moderately useful
    c. Not at all useful

13. What are the issues you face during interface with the citizens coming to Mee Seva Centres?

    Ans. ______________________________

Questionnaire to Assess User/Customer Satisfaction with Mee Seva Services

Name of the District:	*Transaction Code:*
Service Centre Code:	*Name of Service:*

I. *Service Delivery Experience at Mee Seva*

1. Where did you get the Mee Seva application form?
    a. Mee Seva portal
    b. Service centre
    c. Government department
    d. Any other location (Domention______________________
2. How long did you wait to get to the counter and submit your form/get your service?____ minutes
3. How many times were you made to visit Mee Seva centre to get your work done?
    a. Once
    b. Twice
    c. Thrice
    d. Four times
    e. More than four times
4. How often were you denied service due to network connectivity/power failures or any other reason during the visit to Mee Seva centre?
    a. Once
    b. Twice
    c. Thrice
    d. Four times
5. Did you pay any money other than the money for physical form for accessing services at the Mee Seva centre?
    a. Yes
    b. No

6. Whom do you approach if you have a problem with accessing services at the Mee Seva centre?
    1. Operator
    2. Manager
    3. Call centre (1100)
    4. Help desk
    5. pmuMeeSeva@gmail.com

II. *Attitude of the Staff*

7. How does staff at the counter treat you while availing services?
    a. Courteously
    b. Fairly okay
    c. Discourteously

III. *Overall Satisfaction*

8. How do you rate the usefulness of Mee Seva Centre?
    1. Good
    2. Okay
    3. Bad

IV. *Service Delivery Preparedness*

9. How did you know about Mee Seva Centre?
    a. Government publicity
    b. Print and media
    c. Friends/Neighbours/Acquaintances
    d. Prior users
    e. Any other, Please mention________________________________

10. How far is the nearest Mee Seva centre located ____km

11. Are you aware of the various services being provided at the Mee Seva centres?
    a. Yes
    b. No

12. How many services generally did you avail from Mee Seva centres?
    a. One
    b. Two
    c. Three

d. Four or five

e. More than five

V. *Personal Information*

13. Name of the user: ____________________________

14. Age: _____ (Years)

15. Educational Qualifications:

    a. Less than 7th class

    b. SSC

    c. Intermediate

    d. Graduate

    e. Post Graduate and above

    f. Will not Reveal

16. Employment status:

    a. Government service

    b. Private service

    c. Self employment/Business

    d. Unemployed

    e. Retired/Homemaker

17. Income details (₹ per month):

    a. Less than 10000

    b. Between 10000-20000

    c. Between 20000-30000

    d. Between 30000-40000

    e. More than 40000

    f. Will not reveal